Other Books by Thom S. Rainer

Vibrant Church (coauthor)
Raising Dad (coauthor)
Simple Church (coauthor)
The Unexpected Journey
Breakout Churches
The Unchurched Next Door
Surprising Insights from the Unchurched
Eating the Elephant (revised edition) (coauthor)
High Expectations
The Every Church Guide to Growth (coauthor)
The Bridger Generation
Effective Evangelistic Churches
The Church Growth Encyclopedia (coeditor)
Experiencing Personal Revival (coauthor)
Giant Awakenings
Biblical Standard for Evangelists (coauthor)
Eating the Elephant
The Book of Church Growth
Evangelism in the Twenty-first Century (editor)

essential
church?
reclaiming a generation of dropouts

Thom S. Rainer and Sam S. Rainer III

PUBLISHING GROUP
Nashville, Tennessee

978-0-8054-4392-9

Published by B&H Publishing Group,
Nashville, Tennessee

Dewey Decimal Classification: 262
Subject Heading: CHURCH \ EX-CHURCH MEMBERS—
CASE STUDIES \ YOUNG ADULTS

All Scripture quotations are taken from the Holman Christian
Standard Bible®. Copyright © 1999, 2000, 2002, 2003
by Holman Bible Publishers. Used by permission. Holman
Christian Standard Bible®, Holman CSB®, and HCSB® are fed-
erally registered trademarks of Holman Bible Publishers.

1 2 3 4 5 6 7 8 9 10 • 12 11 10 09 08

From Thom

To
Erin Rainer
Sarah Rainer
Rachel Rainer

God's gifts of wives to my sons
God's gifts of daughters-in-law to Nellie Jo and me

And always
To my wife

Love grows where Nellie Jo goes

From Sam

To Erin
My wife
My love
My joy
My anchor

Contents

Acknowledgments

From Thom

I wrote an unpublished paper less than a year ago. Its simple title was "When the Sons Surpass the Father." Since there was really no proper place to publish it, I placed it in a computer file. That was fine. It did not need to be published; it was just an exercise of the heart. But on the occasion of this book, I will cite a portion of that paper:

> Anyone who has heard me speak or read anything
> I wrote knows how much I adore my three sons,
> Sam, Art, and Jess. They have become wonderful
> grown men blessed with three wonderful wives:
> Erin, Sarah, and Rachel.
>
> And it just occurred to me recently: Even though
> they are still young men in their twenties, they have
> surpassed their father already in character, intellect,
> and godliness. Such is a statement of reality and not
> false humility.

The sons have surpassed the father.
I don't deserve them.
Another gift of grace.

I watched with amazement as Sam did the research and writing for this book. I saw his keen mind in action. I saw his heart for the church and lost humanity break with compassion. And I saw his humility as he refused to take credit for a book that is largely his.

The sons have surpassed the father.

His brothers, Art and Jess, are no less amazing. Bright men. Men of integrity. Godly men.

The sons have surpassed the father.

And what wonderful women they brought into their lives and, thus, into our lives. I love Erin Rainer. I love Sarah Rainer. I love Rachel Rainer. I never realized how much I could love daughters-in-law. But I do.

Of course, my sons learned that lesson well—the lesson on how to marry above one's self. We four boys know the truth. The true strength of our family was always their mom and my wife. Nellie Jo Rainer is simply the most wonderful and most beautiful woman in the world. Her unconditional and sacrificial love for all of us is one of the greatest gifts we could ever have.

I simply acknowledge that, if I have ever attained anything worthy of note, it is for two reasons. I have three sons, three daughters-in-law, and a wife who have given me love and honor I don't deserve. And I have a Savior who gave me grace when I deserved judgment.

It is about His church that we write in this book.

From Sam

I must first thank my father and coauthor, Thom Rainer. Dad, thanks for all the guidance, encouragement, and insight. Your fatherly support during the crafting of this book was no different from any other endeavor in my life. You've never told me, "You can't do it." Conversely, you've always said, "I *know* you can do it." Thanks for your confidence and wisdom. Thanks for teaching me the way to go. I'll never depart from it.

This book would never have materialized if it were not for one incredible woman. Erin, my wife, you are gracious beyond measure. Thank you for allowing me the time to write during our first year of marriage. I am blessed to be inspired by your smile, a smile that brightens the world. The joy of Christ radiates from you. I love you so deeply.

I could never have reached where I stand today if it were not for my mother. Mom, thanks so much for championing me. Even the details of this book did not escape your watchful eye. No one else on the planet wants the best for me as you do.

My brothers, Art and Jess, were also great sources of encouragement and honesty. Thanks, bros, for holding me accountable and keeping me down to earth. You keep me laughing through life, through the good and the bad.

The LifeWay Research team and Ed Stetzer clearly laid much of the groundwork for this book. I am grateful for their selfless efforts to provide clarity for our churches through sound research. I am deeply appreciative of Thomas Walters and B&H Publishing Group. Thanks for your patience, kindness, and generosity.

To all my fellow pastors and lay leaders guiding churches to become essential, thank you for your kingdom work. May we always pursue as our goal the prize promised by our heavenly calls in Christ Jesus (see Phil. 3:14).

Most importantly, I write to further the One who grants all blessings. I am mere clay. I pray the Potter is glorified in the writing of this book. After all, it is His church. I am His child. We serve a risen Savior. And for that one reason alone, I am eternally grateful.

Introducing the Essential Church

John Rawls is a successful attorney living the good life in Naples, Florida. He became a full partner five years ago, and he never has a shortage of well-paying clients. In the eyes of many, John is successful. His home is in a pricey, gated community within walking distance of the white beaches of Naples and the beautiful emerald water of the Gulf of Mexico. His children attend an upscale private school, and his wife seems to have no shortage of material comforts.

But John told us that he is not happy.

Despite meeting every apparent criterion of success in the world's eyes, he has a nagging frustration, something he coins "a black hole of emptiness." It was easy to move the conversation to spiritual matters from this point.

Tell us, we said, about your beliefs about God and church. Tell us something about your spiritual background. The floodgates of conversation opened.

"I was raised in a Christian home," he said softly. "My parents were raised Southern Baptists, but they moved to Tampa and joined a nondenominational church. They started taking me to that church when I was in preschool. I still have many great memories of the church."

Do you attend church now?

John swallowed hard for a second and then gave us his story about becoming a church dropout.

"I stopped attending church between the summer of my junior and senior years of high school. I then went on to college and didn't attend church," he admitted. "It's been more than fifteen years, and I still haven't been back."

John is one of millions of "dechurched" Americans. By that we mean that he attended church regularly for years but then joined the growing ranks of unchurched Americans.

"Nothing big or negative caused me to stop attending church," he reflected. "I just came to a point that I did not see church as essential to my life. And I guess that has been the case for more than fifteen years now."

"I did not see church as essential to my life."

Similar statements have been made by millions of dechurched Americans. Church is not essential to their lives. What were the precipitating factors that, in just a few decades, caused churches to move from essential to nonessential in the lives of millions? That is the question that became the basis for this book and our research.

We began a quest for the essential church.

Our journey started with a study of eighteen- to thirty-year-old adults in America. These young adults attended a Protestant church regularly for at least a year while they were in high school. Here is the incredible but sad finding of this study: *More than two-thirds of young churchgoing adults in America drop out of church between the ages of eighteen and twenty-two!*

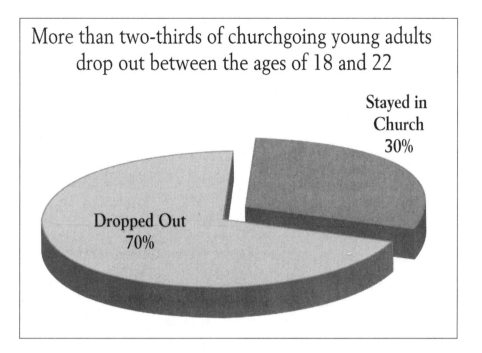

More than two-thirds of churchgoing young adults drop out between the ages of 18 and 22

Stayed in Church 30%

Dropped Out 70%

Why Did They Leave?

We will explore this issue more fully in the first section of this book. For now, let's hear from the dropouts. Look at the ten most common reasons the dechurched said they left the church between the ages of eighteen and twenty-two.

Top Ten Reasons Church Dropouts Stopped Attending Church

1. Simply wanted a break from church.
2. Church members seemed judgmental or hypocritical.
3. Moved to college and stopped attending church.
4. Work responsibilities prevented me from attending.
5. Moved too far away from the church to continue attending.
6. Became too busy though still wanted to attend.
7. Didn't feel connected to the people in my church.
8. Disagreed with the church's stance on political or social issues.

9. Chose to spend more time with friends outside the church.

10. Was only going to church to please others.

We listed these top ten reasons early so you could see a common theme among most of the dropouts. Stated simply, they just did not see that church was essential to their lives. For example, the first reason, cited by 27 percent of the church dropouts, clearly depicts the nonessential attitude of the dropouts toward church: "I simply wanted a break from church."

But even reason number eight, a disagreement with the church on political or social issues, indicates a noncommittal posture. In this case the dropouts easily could have found another church that was a better fit with their social or political views. Instead, they decided to drop out from church totally.

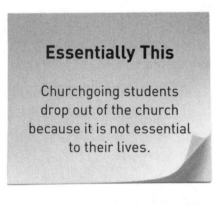

Essentially This

Churchgoing students drop out of the church because it is not essential to their lives.

We looked at the dropout phenomenon of young adults as our study basis. Most church leaders know anecdotally that they lose many active members during the critical years of eighteen to twenty-two. Our research confirmed that perception. Indeed, the fact that the dropout rate was 70 percent surprised us. We found that young adults, when they get to a place where they are making their own decisions about church and other matters, turn away from the church in droves. We cited their top ten reasons for doing so. Are these legitimate reasons? Can the church do anything to reverse this trend?

Stemming the Tide

Imagine a scenario where every church in America more than doubled its worship attendance in one week. And imagine that the increase was sustained with an influx of regenerate, dedicated members.

We estimate that, on a given Sunday, about 85 million people in America attend a Protestant church. What would the spiritual impact on our nation look like if that number suddenly increased to more than 150 million?

That is the exciting scenario we would witness if our churches could stem the tide of exodus of young adults from our churches. And though we are not so naïve as to believe there is a formulaic approach toward this reality, we do believe that some biblical realities could curb this massive exodus.

From Nonessential to Essential Church

Why do more than two-thirds of churchgoing young adult Americans leave the church? Or to ask the question positively, why do one-third of churchgoing young adult Americans stay in the church? The answer to the latter question emerged from several years of research. *Young adults are likely to stay in the church if they see church as essential to their lives.*

Such an answer may seem so obvious that it does not merit much discussion. But the reality is that most churches in America are doing little to become essential to the lives of their members. Indeed, church is seen by most young adults today as but one option among many for their lives. It is no more important than work, leisure activities, or simply doing nothing.

The good news is that we have found churches that are retaining their young adult members. These churches have communicated clearly that the local church is essential to the lives of Christians. They have demonstrated biblically the New Testament reality that God intended for local congregations to gather, worship, disciple, minister, and evangelize. Their church members see the local congregation as a biblical fellowship that they deem critical for their lives.

We call these congregations *essential churches*.

This book takes a simple path. In the first section we look at the disturbing phenomenon of church dropouts, focusing on those who dropped out between the ages of eighteen and twenty-two. In the second section of the book, we demonstrate the types of churches that do not lose these young adults as faithful churchgoers.

The essential church has four major components.

First, the church has learned to **simplify.** Eric Geiger and Thom wrote an entire book about this reality, *Simple Church.* Too many churches are filled with activities that have little coherent purpose. They have no clear process or structure for making disciples, in obedience to the Great Commission of Matthew 28:19–20.

Second, the church moves its members to **deepen** their knowledge of God's Word and His truths. These congregations have resisted the temptation to "dumb down" biblical teachings in an attempt to draw a crowd or to avoid tough issues.

Third, the church has high **expectations** of its members. Most sports teams and civic organizations expect more of their members than churches do. And when expectations are low, commitment is low. The high-expectation church expects much and, thus, receives much from its members. As a result, the church exodus is minimized.

Fourth, an essential church is committed to helping its members **multiply** spiritually. Evangelism is part of the heartbeat of the church. Missions and ministry are common in the lives of the members, and many of these essential churches seek to plant other churches.

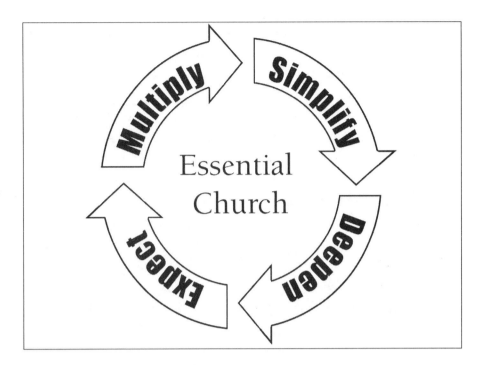

In short, the essential church focuses on four critical areas:

1. Simplify—Get the structure right.
2. Deepen—Get the content right.
3. Expect—Get the attitude right.
4. Multiply—Get the action right.

Can the essential church really reverse the exodus of young adult churchgoers from our congregations? Not only do we believe it's possible; we know of several churches that are doing so today. We will examine in depth the essential church in the second half of this book. For now, let us return to the issue of church dropouts as reflected in the dismal state of the churches in America.

The Decline of the American Church

People leave the church. Pastors and lay leaders alike know this simple fact well. A myriad of books and articles decry the current state of American churches. The outcry from the evangelical world sounds like a broken record; we've all heard the same tape over and over again. Most churches are dwindling. Most denominations are not growing. The population in the United States is exploding, recently surpassing the three hundred million mark. But the church is losing ground. We are in a steep state of decline.

The American church is dying. Conversions are declining in almost every denomination. Even in some of the more relatively healthy denominations, conversions to Christianity have stagnated. In our own denomination, the Southern Baptist Convention (SBC), which is one of the largest Protestant denominations in the world, baptisms have not increased in decades. Despite the growth of the nation, the SBC is baptizing no more people today than it did in 1950.[1]

Worse yet, the church is losing influence in culture. Local churches are having trouble relating to their local community and the younger generation. While some peg this irrelevance as the major underlying factor of declining churches, we believe that it is merely symptomatic of a much greater issue: the church is no longer essential to people's lives. Unless a dramatic change occurs, the American church will continue down the same path as the European church, which is all but dead.

While some churches are thriving, many churches are floundering. The average church is losing the younger generation, and those young adults are not returning. Churches that once were growing are now stagnant. County-seat churches that once were the gathering point for entire communities are now half empty with only gray heads during worship.

How colossal is the problem? Let's take a few steps back in order to grasp the enormity of the issue on a national scale. Clearly individual churches have unique stories. But an understanding of the macro perspective leads to a better diagnosis and path forward for the one church seeking to reverse course.

Looking at the health of the church from the thirty-thousand-foot level, the current state of affairs does not bode well for the future.

If you were to take a peek at the membership rolls of several established churches, a common theme would emerge. What you would find is this: in general, the membership rolls of churches are substantially larger than the average attendance on any given Sunday. In other words, people claim a church, but they do not attend regularly. At some point in the past, they joined and were active. But then they simply stopped attending.

On a national scale the problem of church dropouts is pervasive. The *CIA World Factbook* reports that 52 percent of the population claims a Protestant church.[2] That's a whopping 157 million people as of the date of this writing. How many of these people *really* attend church? Only about 28 percent of the United States' population attends a Protestant church.[3] So, while 157 million people claim a Protestant church, only about 85 million actually attend that church. As we stated before, if all the church dropouts came back next Sunday, Protestant church attendance would double across the nation.

Many of us may have been part of a conversation like this one at some point.

"Hey, Erik, I've known you since your family moved in across the street about three years ago. I've been meaning to ask you, do you have a church home?"

"Sure do."

"Oh really, which one?"

"I'm a member of North End Church."

"I didn't realize that. What part of the church are you involved in?"

"Well, I must admit, Chuck, I haven't been there since the Easter service two years ago."

Exchanges like the one between Chuck and Erik are not shocking to us because they are common. More people choose any number of activities over church attendance. They remain as church members. They even claim the church as their own. But they do not go. The spread between church membership and church attendance is growing. And reaching this segment of dropouts remains a tough task because they use their membership at a church as a conversation stopper. Those who drop out for significant time periods know that when others start to ask them about attending church, they can douse the heat by stating they are members at another church.

Ecclesiastes 1:9 reveals, "What has been is what will be, and what has been done is what will be done; there is nothing new under the sun." This phenomenon of dropouts is no exception. Charles Spurgeon, famed pastor of London's Metropolitan Tabernacle in the late 1800s, wrote the following in his book, *The Soul Winner*:

> In the next place, we do not consider soul-winning to
> be accomplished by hurriedly inscribing more names
> upon our church-roll, in order to show a good increase
> at the end of the year. This is easily done, and there
> are brethren who use great pains, not to say arts, to
> effect it; but if it be regarded as the Alpha and Omega
> of a minister's efforts, the result will be deplorable.[4]

Without a doubt, many churches have quelled the practice of inflated membership. Others are working diligently to remedy the problem while still others are examining ways to reclaim their dropouts. Some churches want to solve the dropout issue but do not know where to begin. No doubt, a slice of churches are making strides to close the back door, but from a national perspective the scale of the problem looms like a dark cloud over our churches. It is not a new problem, but the issue gains weight with each passing year.

We need not look any farther than the Western European church to understand what happens when the church dropout issue hits its final end. Despite a spotty renaissance in some regions due to an influx of immigrants bringing devout beliefs, in most European countries less than 5 percent of the population steps foot in a church except for funerals.[5]

Any traveler to Western Europe will marvel at two aspects of the local churches: how intricately and monstrously beautiful they are as well as how empty they are of parishioners. From Westminster Abbey in London to Notre Dame in Paris, churches built to point glory to God now contain a massive and constant flow of herding tourists. These churches are relevant to their community only in that people, locals and visitors alike, use their premises for a nice place to eat lunch. Many tourists to these churches are shocked and frustrated to find out that they actually have to wait and remain quiet for the few services that still take place with the remnant of loyal churchgoers. For centuries these European churches stood as the focal point and heartbeat of the local community. They now are the focal point and hub of the local tourist industry.

Believers in the United States should not make the assumption that we are free and clear from this dilemma. In fact, we are just a little further behind on the road of irrelevancy. The European church is a harbinger of continued decline in the American church if our churches continue to be nonessential.

Not only is the problem of church dropouts an age-old dilemma that spans across the Atlantic, the problem has worsened here in the United States over the last twenty-five years. From the period of 1990 to 2004, the United States population expanded by more than 18 percent.[6] During this same period the percentage of people attending church declined by about 3 percent.[7] Not only is the church not keeping up with population increases; it is losing ground. In fact, Hawaii is the only state in the union that experienced church growth that outpaced the population growth during the first five years of the new millennium. The rest of the forty-nine states saw declines in church growth relative to the population increases.[8]

The rapid nature of the American church decline in the last three decades rings a loud alarm bell. Are we really paying attention? Or do we think that the problem will solve itself? It will not. Before improvement occurs, individual churches need revivals among their people. The problem exists on a national scale. But the solution remains with each church on a local level. Individual churches must champion the cause on their own. These churches must make a decision to become essential in the lives of their congregation and community. This book doesn't contain all the answers. But we hope that it will be an invaluable tool for helping your church shift from nonessential to essential.

Losing the Battle for a Generation

Travis was a bit reluctant to talk. He is a hefty construction worker from Louisville, Kentucky, with a shaved head, three earrings, and a crooked smile. While we found him to have a rough exterior, he is a teddy bear inside. He claimed to be a Christian.

We had started the conversation with small talk about the upcoming college football season. The twenty-seven-year-old is a die-hard University of Kentucky football fan. He rarely misses a chance to watch the Cats play, whether he watches them on television or goes to Commonwealth Stadium in Lexington. He remains an undeterred optimist about the potential of his beloved Wildcats. Despite the lackluster performance from the middle-tier football school, Travis keeps his hopes high for the future. They may not have done so well last year, but he knows this year is the year for the Cats.

Then we asked him about his church.

"My church?" His tone changed quickly. And his end of the conversation shifted from passion to reluctance.

"Yes, Travis, tell us about your church."

"Not much to say, I guess."

"Which area church do you attend?"

"Depends."

"Do you go anywhere on a regular basis?"

"Not really. I guess I left my old church about nine years ago. To be perfectly honest, I could never find a church that I was passionate about. My church was good for me when I was a child, but now I just don't feel like I can plug in anywhere. I don't like wishy-washiness and flaky worship. If there was a church out there that was real, up-front, and in-your-face about what really needs to happen in your life, then I might give it a shot."

"You haven't written off church then?" We were trying to get to the heart of why he stopped attending church.

"Not at all." Travis was beginning to open up. "My parents went to church mostly. My grandparents were there three times a week. Everyone in my family is a Christian. I even went to a Christian school for a while. So I guess I really don't have much of an excuse. But when I commit to something, it's all or nothing. I'm a loyal-to-the-bone kind of guy. I don't do anything half-hearted. All the churches I ever went to didn't have a place for me. I mean, it's not like they make eighteen-year-olds deacons or anything. I just didn't want to wait around to serve, so I left."

"I just didn't want to wait around to serve, so I left."

Maybe it was the earrings. Maybe it was Travis's sometimes gruff demeanor. But for whatever reason his church didn't make a place for him to serve.

I think we all know someone like Travis—somewhat of a loose cannon but also someone you can count on for anything. People like him make loyal friends. They are the ones helping you load up your U-Haul when you move. They are the ones showing up at the hospital for your outpatient surgery. They are the ones replacing the brakes on your car to help save you a buck or two.

Churches desperately need people like Travis. But the church remains unattractive to them. The church let Travis head right out the back door. And he feels like he isn't the slightest bit missed. After the interview, we wondered if his previous church even knew he existed.

Scores of stories like Travis's story are floating around among the dropouts. Their grandparents were at the church every time the doors opened. Their parents went regularly but not as often. Then the children and grandchildren grow up in church and fall away between the ages of eighteen and twenty-two.

In our research this trend was perhaps the most disturbing. What we uncovered was a downward spiral of not only church dropouts but also people who claim Christ. Perhaps most startling is the gravity of how many exit the church and the pace at which this exodus is occurring. Each generation that passes loses more than the previous generation. Shock does not begin to describe how we felt after reading the research results. The church is losing the generational battle. Not only are we losing our nation to the ways of the world, but we are not winning our own children in Christian families. Multitudes are dropping out of church. But many are also not claiming the faith of their parents.

In Ephesians 6, Paul details each piece of spiritual armor that Christians are to wear. We fight for souls. We battle to win our children for Christ. The church should present a unified front so that we can stand firm against the powers of this world. We fear that many churches have placed their armor in the closet. Or they buff it up in order to show it off like a new car.

Armor is not meant to be shiny. Armor is meant to be used in battle. This armor should have dings, scratches, scuffs, and dents in it. It is not our armor. It is the Lord's armor. And the Lord has promised our churches final victory. We fight in this battle knowing that we are the victors. But our churches must cooperate for the sake of the gospel and winning the next generation for Christ. With the downward spiral of dropouts occurring at such an alarming rate, we wonder if the vast majority of churches are even on the battlefield, much less on the front lines.

Reversing this trend will not come easy. The enemy is well entrenched. But putting on the armor of God and fighting this spiritual battle is a necessity for the survival of the church. Most are aware of the fact that people leave the church. Most understand that we are losing the generational battle. The question we answer next is, at what point does this battle become hottest? When do most dropouts leave?

Unsweet Sixteen

The generational battle reaches a flash point when teens reach the age of sixteen. This critical juncture of a young person's life is where the church begins to lose the majority of people in the battle over generations. As the chart below details, what became clearly evident through our research is that most of the dropouts leave the church between the ages of seventeen and nineteen.[9]

Percentage gain/loss for age categories in the church	
Between 15 and 16	+1%
Between 16 and 17	-15%
Between 17 and 18	-24%
Between 18 and 19	-29%
Between 19 and 20	-5%

These losses are considerable. In just three short years of a teen's life, he or she makes the decision to leave the church. By age twenty-one, most dropouts are basically already gone. In order to stop the mass exodus, churches must renew their focus on those in the mid to late teens. While the church must remain focused on the discipleship of people of all ages, someone celebrating their sweet sixteen in your church should make you evaluate where that teen stands spiritually. Indeed, essential churches begin the discipleship process even earlier in a child's life.

We began this chapter by introducing the essential church. We then detailed the unhealthiness of our churches on a national scale and revealed how churches are losing the generational battle. Next we will reveal several aspects of nonessential churches. What does a nonessential church look like? Certain commonalities exist among those churches that are not reaching the next generation. In the next section we will describe seven sins of dying churches that are the driving factors behind losing the generational battle.

Seven Sins of Dying Churches

The age-old adage rings true for churches: if you are not moving forward, then you are moving backward. Stagnation equates to dying. Your church may look the same week in and week out, but if you are not winning the next generation for Christ, then you are losing the battle. We will categorize some of the more prevalent transgressions that dying churches commit. These seven sins are not mutually exclusive and are often interconnected. The list is not exhaustive, but we almost always observe some combination of these sins in dying churches.

Sin 1. Doctrine Dilution

Certain absolutes found within Scripture are so crucial that a Christian should be willing to sacrifice his or her life for them. Cardinal truths such as the exclusivity of Christ must be followed if the American church is to survive this evangelistic crisis. Watering down Scripture is not the answer to reaching a younger generation for Christ. They do not want to be mollycoddled with tough doctrinal truths. Teaching anything less than the absolute truths in Scripture will make the younger generation feel betrayed when they learn that a large gap exists between what the Bible *really* says and what they were taught in church. Diluting the truth to cater to eighteen- to twenty-two-year-olds may work for a time, but low-dose Christianity stings the church much worse in the long run.

Sin 2. Loss of Evangelistic Passion

Dying churches have little evangelistic passion. They putter around in sharing their faith. When Peter and John faced the tribunal in Acts 4, the accusers were amazed at the boldness of their faith. When the tribunal demanded silence and ordered them not to preach and teach the name of Jesus or else face losing their lives, Peter and John responded, "We are unable to stop speaking about what we have seen and heard" (v. 20). Dying churches stop speaking about Christ to the world. Evangelistic fervor becomes apathetic disinterest in a lost world.

As we will see later in the book, much responsibility rests upon the leadership of the church. It is the responsibility of the pastor and other key leaders to exhibit this evangelistic passion. In many thriving churches the driving force behind obedience to the Great Commission is the passion that the senior pastor maintains for the lost. This passion will flow from the top down. As the congregation sees his zeal, they catch the same fire.

Sin 3. Failure to Be Relevant

Relevance is a buzzword among churches today. We believe that it is a good one. And there is nothing more relevant to a lost world than the saving grace of Jesus Christ. The unchanging truths of Scripture will always contain the answer for those searching to fill the void of their lives. The church, however, must find ways to relay this gospel message to the culture around them. The church in a farming community in Indiana should relate differently from the church in a suburb of Vancouver, which should relate differently from the church in the heart of New York City. Churches that do not find ways to become relevant in their respective communities will eventually falter. Churches that keep their internal culture unchanged for fifty years while the world around them goes through continual periods of metamorphosis typically die with that old culture. Churches that ask the question, "How can we best relate the unchanging gospel to the shifting culture around us?" are one step closer to relevancy and reaching a new generation.

Sin 4. Few Outwardly Focused Ministries

"It's all about me!" is the anthem chant of the dying church. As crucial as Bible studies and fellowship are, dying churches gorge themselves on closed study groups and churchwide fellowship events while neglecting outreach in the community. The country club church can remain so for a limited amount of time. In order for the American church to survive, it must reach into the community with outwardly focused ministries. Dying churches heavily skew their ministries internally. Essential churches think outward into the surrounding communities and into the world, earnestly seeking ways to win the next soul for Jesus.

Sin 5. Conflict over Personal Preferences

Are the bulletins supposed to be trifold or bifold? What type of font is better suited for the newsletter, Arial or Times New Roman? Pews, seats, or sofas? Do we serve rotgut coffee or shell out the big bucks for Arabian Mocha Sanani? People within the church can squabble over the most insignificant things. And these internal conflicts smother a church. These quibbles overshadow the true purpose of the church. When the church focuses on trivial matters, the greater gospel message is left on the sidelines. Essential churches grasp the primacy of the gospel. Languishing churches are mired in conflict over paltriness.

When the power of personal preference overcomes the calling of the Great Commission, major myopia spreads among the congregation. They do not see the imperative to win people for Christ due to the blurriness of their own selfishness. The essential church breaks through the quagmire of personal preference and unites the people around the common causes of spiritual growth and missions.

Sin 6. The Priority of Comfort

Dying churches are comfortable with their ministries. They do nothing outside the bounds of their comfort levels. Church members do not come to the leadership with reservations about the next ministry goal because they are not spiritually stretched. People in dying churches choose their priority of comfort over reaching beyond the church bubble into a community full of specific and difficult needs.

But "the way we've always done it" will not pass muster if the American church is to thrive. Churches that flourish get outside comfort zones and reach into areas that are uncharted for them. "We've never done that before" is typically followed by, "but we'll do what it takes to fulfill our calling as a church." Essential churches hunker down and prepare to get uncomfortable in following God's call. Dying churches refuse to stretch beyond their limited zones of comfort.

Sin 7. Biblical Illiteracy

We are to be diligent to present ourselves to God, workers not needing to be ashamed, correctly teaching the word of truth (see 2 Tim. 2:15). One of the major sins of a dying church is the neglect of theological teaching. If a church member does not understand the basics of Scripture, then they are hampered in their witness. Those who do not comprehend the Scriptures will also have trouble remaining obedient. Biblical illiteracy runs rampant in floundering churches. Since the people of the church do not understand the foundation of their faith, they stand on shaky ground and falter during the first time of trouble.

Defining the Terms

Before we proceed further, we feel it is prudent to define several terms that will be used in the book. Five words, in particular, will be used frequently. The first term, *dropouts*, refers to those who left the church between the ages of eighteen and twenty-two. A second term, *dechurched*, refers to everyone, in general, who once was part of a local congregation but has since neglected the fellowship of the church. Those who are *unchurched* do not belong to a church. This term is more general in nature. It can include both those who once attended a church and those who have never stepped foot inside a sanctuary. *Outsiders*, like *unchurched*, refers to those who do not attend a church, and they have no connection to a church. The last term, *rechurched*, denotes the group of people who once were unchurched but have since returned to a local body of believers.

Becoming an Essential Church

Churches that close the back door share several commonalities. The overarching component to their success: the church is essential to the lives of the people. Members of essential churches do not have an easy way out. The church becomes such a vital part of their lives that neglecting the fellowship of believers is not a painless option.

While these churches share some similarities, they all look different. Essential churches come in different sizes, polities, venues, and styles. The reason for such a variety of essential churches is simple: they major on the majors and minor on the minors. They don't jump on the latest fads, nor do they become bogged in the quagmire of unnecessary traditions.

Becoming an essential church is not the easiest of paths. Some churches may have to slaughter a sacred cow. Others may need to refocus their entire mission. Others may have to tweak certain ministries. If you are a pastor or lay leader reading this book, please realize that we cannot and will not tell you exactly how your church must look. The church is indeed a "profound mystery" (Eph. 5:32). But while it may take several shapes, forms, styles, and sizes, the one thing that a church must be is essential. A nonessential church is a dying church.

The dismal reality is that the vast majority of churches have become nonessential. The church in the United States sits in the doldrums, going nowhere. With more than 80 percent of North American churches stagnant or declining, the church is quickly becoming nonessential to society. With nearly four thousand churches closing their doors permanently each year, a turnaround is imperative.[10]

The church in America is in a state of decline. We cannot ignore the brutal facts. Too many churches are nonessential. The vast majority of churches don't become essential in the lives of their congregants and community. Regardless, we remain optimistic. We believe firmly that faith the size of a mustard seed still moves mountains. We also believe that the church can make a dramatic turnaround.

No cookie-cutter formula exists. Each church reaches a unique community. But we believe the four-phase essential model applies to any church. **Simplify**—the church develops a clear structure and process for making disciples. **Deepen**—the church provides strong biblical teaching and preaching. **Expect**—the church has an attitude that communicates to its members that they must be committed to the local congregation. **Multiply**—the church has an outward focus, driving to reach people for Christ and starting new churches.

A nationwide church boom is desperately needed. Our national population recently soared past 300 million. The minority population crossed the 100 million mark for the first time ever.[11] The harvest is waiting. The fields are ripe with people waiting to hear the gospel. Our churches must respond. They must become essential.

PART 1

Why People Leave the Nonessential Church

CHAPTER 1

My Faith Is Not My Parents' Faith

Joe chuckled at the question, but we could tell it made him uneasy. Up until this point in our interview, the conversation was lighthearted. Joe bragged about his children, his wife, and his family in East Tennessee. He's a clean-cut, corporate guy, but we were surprised to hear he wanted to be a rock star as a young adult. Apparently his father didn't take too kindly to his vain attempts for a rock 'n' roll mane. Today he helps to lead music for his church's praise and worship team. Joy, love, and passion exude from him; his commitment to his church is readily apparent.

Such was not always the case in Joe's life. Joe was a church dropout for many years. Asking him about this segment of his life clearly evoked difficult memories.

"I truly believe I had a genuine conversion experience when I was eleven, but when I went to college, I wanted to be as far from my church as possible."

We asked him what happened.

"I was a shy child and teenager, never dabbling in anything too horribly rebellious. In fact, I was very much an introvert—that is, until I turned eighteen."

"What was the turning point?"

Joe continued, "I guess since the church was never a critical element of my life, it was easier to leave. When I woke up to my own personality as a young adult, I wanted nothing more than to pursue the world and its pleasures. I went from a quiet child to a rebellious adult seeking sin to its greatest degrees."

"What did your parents say and do when you made this decision?"

Joe choked up. "They always asked me to return to church. I went through so many struggles, yet I never viewed my local church as an option for help. Quite frankly, the church wasn't the same for me as it was for them."

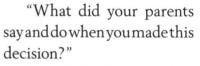

Essentially This

Students are not fleeing the church because of deep desires for personal freedom.

We interrupted his stream of comments and focused on this element of his church. We asked, "Why was your church different for you?"

"I guess I never saw how my faith and my church connected. I knew I was saved. I knew I was sinning. I felt convicted about living this lifestyle. But I didn't see how it all tied in to the church."

"I guess I never saw how my faith and my church connected."

Joe is like so many who drop out of the church. We heard a myriad of reasons and excuses for leaving the church, but one predominant theme was that eighteen- to twenty-two-year-olds did not see their faith like their parents' faith. The church connection was somehow lost with the younger generation.

We heard Joe talk at length about his parents, how they continued to love him and reach out to him during this time in his life. But their reason for going back to church was simply, "You need to get back in church."

This line of conviction and argumentation perhaps worked with older generations, but it does not resonate with the latest generation of young adults. This generation likes to talk about faith. Many believe, rightly or wrongly, that they *have* faith. Religious matters do not scare them. Most maintain some level of interest in spiritual topics. But unless this generation fuses faith and church, they will see no reason to stay in church. Frankly, the faith of their parents is not reason enough for them to claim it as their own.

Our research revealed what many pastors and church leaders already know anecdotally: the youngest generation doesn't necessarily leave their faith; rather they leave their church. This finding was both encouraging and frightening. On the one hand, the eighteen- to twenty-two-year-old age group maintains at least some level of receptivity to issues of spirituality. On the other hand, they disconnect this spirituality from their church. They aren't dropping their faith. But they are dropping the church.

The Myth of Freedom

A credit card company advertises their "freedom card." While we think it perverse that a company would advertise a vehicle for debt as freedom, we will use it as an illustration anyway. In the commercials they use an old Rolling Stones tune that goes, "I'm free to do what I want . . . any old time." Now that you have the song stuck in your head, we want to discuss a myth about high school students and church. The myth: young church dropouts leave the fellowship because of their desire for personal freedom. The truth is the opposite.

Let's debunk this myth up front. Most students in high school *do not plan to leave the church.* In fact, our research reveals that an overwhelming majority (80 percent) of high school students do not plan to leave their church once they graduate.[1] Conversely, only 20 percent of high school students have plans to leave their local church once they are out of their parents' nest.

This finding contradicts what is commonly believed within the church: college students do not attend church because they are sowing their wild oats and enjoying newfound freedom away from home. It's simply not true. By and large, high school students do not have a deep desire to leave the church.

We talked to a high school senior who decided to leave his small town to go to a flight school in Florida. We asked him about his decision and how he felt about it.

"I'm excited about getting an opportunity to fulfill my dreams of becoming a pilot," he said, "but I do have some reservations."

"Like what?"

"Well, I'll miss my family, of course. But I'll also miss all the people at my church. I've had a great time getting to learn all the sound equipment and helping out during the service. I'll definitely miss doing that every week."

This student went on to tell us how his church had trained him starting in junior high to be one of the main people on the sound crew. He took ownership in what he did for the church. He knew that he contributed to what the church was trying to accomplish. He knew that he was a critical component of the body of believers. The fact that he was not able to continue contributing to his home church on a regular basis pained him.

From our data we can infer anecdotally that one substantial reason many do not plan to leave is because their church is taking an active role in their lives. In other words, the church is essential to them because they know that they are essential to the church, even at a young age.

The myth of freedom is debunked. Churches should not place all the blame on the students for exiting the church. While students are certainly accountable for their own actions, the church also has the responsibility to make students a valued part of ministry. The church always has an array of responsibilities in need of filling—sound and lighting, greeters, preschool workers, and parking attendants, among many other tasks. Give them a note card with pertinent information on it and let them make the church announcements. Allow them to pray during the service. Train those that are more spiritually mature to teach in small groups of elementary school children. An essential church uses all believers in the church for service, including students. These students are not looking for freedom; they desire responsibility. Put them to the task and watch them grow.

Not Losing My Religion

As a Southern colloquialism, "losing my religion" does not refer to a departure from one's faith but rather a loss of civility and lack of control over anger. We title this section "Not Losing My Religion" because church dropouts are neither angry at the church nor casting off their religion. They are not losing their religion, but quietly and without emotion they exit the local church.

In Mark 4:1–20, Jesus teaches through the parable of the sower. This passage illustrates how seeds of equal value fall on different types of soil. The main emphasis of this portion of Scripture is not the sowing action or the seeds but rather the condition of the soil. Two types of soil exist: productive and unproductive. The unproductive seeds are scattered in thorns, fall on rocky soil, and are strewn about every place except in the good soil. What makes the seed productive is the type of soil in which it lies. We fear this study exposes that there are many young, scattered seeds resting everywhere but on productive soil. As a result the church must refocus to become part of the Lord's eternal and bountiful harvest.

We found the results of this part of our research surprising. Most dropouts are not leaving because they no longer want to identify with organized religion. Dropouts do not all question their faith. Few are angry with or have stopped believing in God. These dropouts don't completely depart from their *faith*. They rather part ways with the *church*. In fact, only 16 percent of dropouts reported that they left their church because they no longer wanted to identify with organized religion.[2] So let's now examine which parts of the church are sources of disillusionment for the younger generation.

The most glaring issue of estrangement for eighteen- to twenty-two-year-olds is the interminable gap between their personal beliefs and their church's stated beliefs. In other words, the church's stated external beliefs, covenant, or confession goes against the personal and internal belief structure of these younger adults. Only 53 percent of all young adult churchgoers state that they are in line with the beliefs of their church.[3] The dropout crisis isn't found in the style, venue, programs, or location of the church. This crisis is much deeper; it runs to the core of the doctrinal truths of the church. Only half of our young adults agree with the church's teachings.

To be blunt, God has *converted* our children, but we have failed to *disciple* them. Our children grow up in the church and experience all the programs and fellowship, but they do not engage the truths of Scripture. When they go to college or find a new social network, the church's role is replaced. They have no need to maintain what they perceive as their parents' social circle now that they have their own.

The mere fact that half of our current young adult population within our churches do not personally align with the doctrinal teachings of the church should sound the alarm for the need to increase our discipleship efforts. With such a divide between the church and the individual, it comes as no surprise that young adults leave the church in masses.

The dropouts are not mad. Many still claim their faith. They can still have a positive view of their pastor and church. They aren't losing their religion. Most just see no reason to stay; the church is not essential to them. It is just another social venue with which they have little in common. Dropouts feel this way because many within the church assumed that they would stay. Their parents assumed that the teachings of the church would be well received via religious osmosis. But the Great Commission explicitly commands us to teach and disciple. Neglecting this element of the gospel imperative creates an atmosphere of spiritual and doctrinal atrophy resulting in a nonessential church.

UCLA's Higher Education Research Institute recently reported through their research that students may be less likely to attend religious services while in college, but this lack of attendance does not mean that they are wrestling with their faith. In fact, after three years of college, students are more engaged in a spiritual quest than they were as freshmen.[4] But during this same time period, college students attend church much less frequently. Among incoming freshmen, 43.7 percent said they frequently attend religious services, but by the end of their junior year attendance was down to 25.4 percent.[5]

During college, interest in religious matters goes up, yet attendance in church falls precipitously. Interest in religion clearly does not equate to believing in the fundamentals of the Christian faith. But the church is not capturing and engaging these students' spiritual interests. In fact, the church is doing the opposite. We're losing them because the church is uninteresting to them.

The major source of disillusionment within the church stems not from the expected differences of worship style wars, time slots, day of worship, or even geographic location of the church. While some do leave for these oft-stated reasons, the major loss originates from the lack of discipleship within our churches.

No doubt, some dropouts leave regardless of the health of the church. Some exit because they renounce their religion, which we address in the next section. Some are angry. Some are looking for a different spin on church. But the vast majority do not lose their religion. They simply lose the church.

Back to the Basics

Sarah was one of our younger interviewees. She was nineteen, and she was actively involved in her local church. She was a greeter in her church. She regularly helped teach the children in Sunday school. And she was typically the first to sign on for mission trips. In fact, the orange T-shirt she was wearing had the church logo on the front and "I love my church!" printed on the back.

We had to ask, "Why do you love your church so much?"

"It's where I was saved and where I grow to be more Christlike."

Basic enough.

Sarah didn't leave her church after her eighteenth birthday. She moved out of her parents' house into a local apartment and is attending the college in her city. But she did not drop out of her church.

What was so essential about her church? It looks like any other church. They have the same struggles as most other churches. They don't have a coffee shop or a dynamic contemporary service. The pastor is not a well-known national religious figure. Sarah's church was essential in her life because Christ was essential in her life.

Our research indicates that a lot of teens and young adults could become active like Sarah. But before they reach that point, the church needs to get back to the basics with them. The church cannot assume that the teens coming with their parents and friends every week are Christians. Indeed, one of the biggest mission fields may be those sitting in your church every week. And the sad reality is that many leave the church because they were not believers in the first place.

Looking for more but not finding it in church. As we wrote this chapter, an Associated Press/MTV poll was released on teen happiness. Surprisingly, for those in the thirteen to twenty-four age range, a high correlation exists between spirituality and happiness. In other words, teens and young adults who are on a spiritual journey are happier than those that are not. In fact, 44 percent of those interviewed stated that religion is very important to them.[6]

This receptivity to spiritual matters is encouraging. The sad news is that most are not Christians. Seven out of ten thirteen- to twenty-four-year-olds in this survey state that while their religion is vital to their lives, other religions and belief systems are probably true as well. Our nation's youth are looking for more in life, but they are not finding it. The spiritual journey makes them happy, but this journey does not lead them to the ultimate fulfillment found in Jesus Christ.

While the above survey includes teens inside and outside of church and focuses on a vague sense of spirituality, our researchers wanted to know how an evangelical church becomes essential in the lives of the younger generation. We see that this generation is seeking something spiritual. What must the church do to connect with them? Perhaps Ed Stetzer of LifeWay Research says it best: "Teens are looking for more from a youth ministry than a holding tank with pizza. They look for a church that teaches them how to live life. As they enter young adulthood, church involvement that has made a difference in their lives gives them a powerful reason to keep attending."[7]

Be encouraged at the receptivity of this age group. But in order to retain them, the church must dig deeper. We must give them something that sticks. The glue that holds them to church isn't a whiz-bang program or an exciting service; the glue is the saving grace of Jesus Christ.

When past experiences collide with future opportunities. Matt smiled when we asked him about his church. You could tell he was dedicated to and loved the people at his place of worship.

"But I wasn't always like this," he said matter-of-factly. Matt worked long hours at a manufacturing plant. His daily commute could easily stretch into an hour one way, depending on traffic.

"When Charlie came along," Matt said, speaking of his preschool-age son, "I wanted to spend all my spare time with him."

"So you sacrificed your time at church to do so?"

"Exactly," he replied.

"When were you convicted to come back?"

"My wife and I just knew that after a couple of years we still had this void in our lives. We weren't going to be good parents feeling the way we did."

"Going back helped fill that void?"

"No, realizing I was neglecting the call of God was the bigger issue. Going back to church wasn't enough. I needed to be the man for my family that God was calling me to be."

"How did you come to this realization?"

Matt looked around the room as he gathered his thoughts. "I don't place any blame on my former church, but I was never challenged personally at the church where I grew up. While I take full responsibility for my actions, I just wish that people had invested more in me personally."

Matt is now a lay leader in his church. His current church challenges him, and he is part of a mentoring group for those working through a call to ministry. He preaches occasionally on Sunday nights. Matt now feels the church is essential to his life. While he still struggles with his work schedule and balancing family life (and who doesn't), the church is a key component of helping him do that.

Like Matt, young adults often drop out of church when they enter into a new phase of life. Going to college, getting a promotion, getting married, or having a child demands more time from an individual. These new opportunities and life changes require an internal evaluation of where and how time will be managed in the future. Since twenty-eight-hour days do not exist (and many of us wish they did), time slots must be shuffled to accommodate the new opportunity or life change. If the church is not an essential component of their life, then the time dedication to a local body of believers is often one of the first to go.

The past experiences of the church with the dropout may not be negative. Churches should not assume that people are leaving acrimoniously. Most do not leave with bitterness. Their past experiences may even be positive. They just view their current opportunity or time constraints as more important than their ties to their local church.

Give me a break! As mentioned in the introduction, the number one reason young adults leave the church is because they simply wanted a break from church. Ingrained in the minds of our youth is the deep-rooted belief that taking a sabbatical from church is permitted and even refreshing.

Church is not a chore, nor should it be viewed as such. Lost somewhere is the idea that we are to grow discipled warriors for God. Church can be fun; fellowship is many times viewed as one of the essential purposes of the church. But our churches should produce and grow disciplined, God-glorifying people, not callow Christians.

Taking a break from church is synonymous with taking a break from God. The two are inexplicably tied—Christ the bridegroom, the church His bride (see Eph. 5:31–33). Regardless of any reason, many of our youth believe that this hiatus from church is worthwhile. And we shouldn't react with disdain but rather with a loving heart that shows them how critical a role church plays in the life of people. Neglecting the fellowship is just not an option (see Heb. 10:25).

At issue in many churches are the vast numbers of programs and "spots to fill." Our youth see adults in the church begrudgingly serving in areas for which they have little passion. They see their parents and others getting sucked into the vacuum of church service. But if we show these young adults that serving the church is more about using their God-given gifts and less about filling a spot in a program, they are less likely to want a break from church.

The people of the church. The Rainer household is a competitive one. My (Sam's) wife, Erin, can almost beat me in tennis . . . almost. But it still drives me crazy. Within the family are graduates from the University of Alabama (my father and coauthor, Thom), the University of South Carolina (Sam), and the University of Kentucky (my younger brother, Art). SEC football reigns supreme in the fall, and we've learned not to call one another after bad defeats. I clearly remember from my childhood how Dad wore our carpet thin pacing during every Alabama football game. Each of his three sons still dislike the Auburn Tigers to this day due to his influence.

Competition was the norm in a household of three boys. So when my two younger brothers devised a Tournament of Champions for my bachelor party, it was no-holds-barred for the group of guys involved. The competition consisted of go-carts, laser tag, air hockey, putt-putt, and pop-a-shot. A scoring matrix was derived for each game, and a detailed list of rules and regulations was distributed. The camouflage and face paint scared the younger children in the arcade. The competition was intense.

Despite the intensity it was a good time to catch up on life's events. I had not seen some of my high school friends in a while so I asked them about their churches and what they were doing in their local body. One of my good friends, Jon, reluctantly answered that he had not attended church in some time. I was somewhat taken aback because Jon was raised in the church and had attended a Christian school. He proclaimed to be born again. I asked Jon why he had stopped attending his local church. He curtly responded with some measure of guilt, "I just don't feel connected to the people anymore."

"I just don't feel connected to the people anymore."

I thought, if Jon (and others like him) could be as intense about his involvement with the local church as he is with our silly Tournament of Champions, then the church would be alive with evangelical energy. Unfortunately though, too many within this young adult age bracket are rapidly leaving the church.

The entire Tournament of Champions crew was in their early to mid-twenties. And this age group had intensity and energy that could be directed at ministries within the church. Our research shows that one of the greatest needs within the young adult generation is building relationships and connecting with one another. Additionally, this group is searching for the truth, and they do not want to be mollycoddled on Sunday morning. They are seeking a challenge. And they value the journey of finding things out for themselves. My friend Jon loves a challenge, and he is one who truly wants to make a difference in other people's lives.

Jon's view of the disconnectedness of church is similar to that of many within our study. The disparity between the dropouts and those who stayed is large. It may sound like common sense, but many times common sense is overlooked. Dropouts left because they felt disconnected from the people of the church; those who stayed did so because they felt connected.

There is a clear correlation between how young adults perceive the people of the church and whether they drop out. In other words, young adults connect to churches where the people are open, positive, and caring. Conversely, young adults drop out of churches where the people are indifferent or critical. The chart following demonstrates this unmistakable divide between the perceptions of the dropouts and those who stayed.

Percent of 18 to 22 year olds who maintain the below impressions about their church[8]		
	Those who stayed	Those who dropped out
Caring	74%	39%
Welcoming	71%	36%
Authentic	67%	30%
Inspirational	56%	20%
Insincere	19%	41%
Judgmental	24%	51%

Each church believes it is the most friendly, caring, and authentic church in town. In reality, it could be the case. But many churches are not perceived as such by the eighteen- to twenty-two-year-old crowd.

An essential church is an authentic church. While young adults want to be welcomed and loved just like anyone else, they also desire authenticity. This generation was born into a marketed world. Streams of commercials, billboards, Web sites, and reality TV are normative in the lives of the wireless generation. They've never seen a rotary dial telephone; they might not even own a landline telephone (Sam and his wife do not). They see through phoniness because it's plastered everywhere they go. They can sniff out artificialness with hound dog accuracy. Whether it's an image, a lifestyle, or a product, they are constantly being sold something.

Taking this same approach with your church is bound to backfire. Churches should not attempt to "sell" this generation on church. They want their church to be authentic and real. They want the truth, even if they disagree with it. They want to know where you stand. They may not like it at first, but they will respect you. And being real always garners respect in the eyes of young adults. An essential church captures this authenticity. An essential church does not attempt to be something it is not. Fanciness may attract a crowd for a while, but assimilation will never occur unless a church is truly authentic, transparent, and real.

The church should be greatly encouraged by the fact that young adults are ready for reality. And we should be training and discipling them, placing them in pertinent leadership roles and holding them accountable. When the bar is set high and excellence is demanded, the church will then attract and keep those who truly seek to assimilate and make a difference in ministry.

But remember that we are not *competing* for the souls of the lost. Rather, we are in battle. We battle the powers of darkness over the eternity of someone's soul. The apostle Paul states in Philippians 4:1 that we are called to stand firm. An essential church keeps a united front, everyone standing shoulder to shoulder, swords in hand, warriors ready to face the enemy. The body of believers needs those who will champion the gospel message, those who will share their faith unwaveringly, and those willing to stand firm.

There are many hills upon which to die. The people of an essential church say they will only die for the fundamentals of the faith. They are a real people, focused on the primacy of the gospel message. They are authentic but willing to change the modes, means, and methods of how they share the unchanging truth of Jesus Christ.

An essential church does not *compete* for sanctuary fillers. An essential church *battles* the dark powers for the hearts and minds of the lost.

The church needs relevant and exciting energy to reach those who do not know Christ. While a person of any age can certainly display such characteristics, an entire younger generation is walking away from the church because they feel their contributions are not appreciated or welcomed. Churches that recapture this young adult group will certainly see an increase in those who desire to be champions for Christ, winning an entire generation for Jesus.

The pastor of the church. One surprising aspect of our research was the critical role that a pastor plays with those under eighteen. And the major connecting point between this age group and the pastor is the sermon.

Meredith is a chirpy twenty-two-year-old with a big smile. Though she just moved to a different town, she told us about her pastor in the church where she grew up and his influence on her when she was in high school.

"I really loved the way he connected with all of us," she said.

"How did he connect with you? Was it a cutting-edge kind of church?"

"No, actually, it was a traditional church in a midsize town. You could say we were one of those churches that hasn't changed much since the 1960s. But the pastor knew how to get to our level in his sermons."

We asked, "What did he do in his sermons to connect so well with the high school group?"

"He *literally* got on our level." She smiled. "He would come down from behind the behemoth wood pulpit and talk directly to us as students."

"He would dedicate portions of his sermons to the youth and address them specifically?"

"Yes, he did. It wasn't every sermon, but I remember his doing it a lot."

"And this connected with you guys?"

She laughed. "Well, we would roll our eyes at times, but inside I think most everyone appreciated the fact that he did that. Looking back on it now and talking about it actually makes me miss that church!"

"Sounds like your pastor made a big impact on you and others through his sermons."

"Yes, he did. There's no doubt about it."

Our research plainly shows that the better a pastor connects with the students of the church through his sermons, the more likely they are to stay in the church. And the sermon disconnect may be larger than you realize. Illustrated in the chart below is the breakdown of dropouts and the pastor's sermons.

Perceptions of the pastor's sermons for those under 18[9]		
	Dropouts	Stayed
The pastor's sermons were engaging.	48%	65%
The pastor's sermons were relevant to me.	42%	63%

The temptation for the pastor to write a sermon for the adult audience is understandable. It is also understandable that many churches leave connecting with the students up to the youth pastor or student minister. But our research illuminates the need for pastors to reach out intentionally to the under-twenty-two age bracket. So the surprising insight here shouldn't be all that surprising: biblical truth must be conveyed to all age groups in the church, not just the adults. It is the pastor's responsibility to communicate this truth in his sermons, even if it means taking a portion of the sermon time to address specific age groups during the service.

Many churches have children's sermons. Why not also speak directly to the youth? In most churches this age group typically sits together. Instead of bemoaning their lack of interest in sermons geared toward adults, engage them with sermons geared specifically for them. Don't assume that their faith is like that of their parents. Be relevant to them on their level. After all, the pastor of the church is also their pastor. They are smart enough to figure that out. If the pastor is not connecting with them, this generation will see it for what it is—a disconnect. Why are we shocked when they leave the church and then cite this disconnect problem as a reason for their departure?

The parents of the church. Not only do the people and pastor of the church have an influence over the student age group, but the parents also play a critical role in the assimilation of teens and college-age young adults. The combined power of parents with the pastor and others in the church can make a big difference in the life of someone under twenty-two.

Parents who attend church with their children help assimilate them in their church. As we will discuss in chapter 4, however, this attendance must be accompanied by spiritual guidance from the parents. We realize that not all students who attend church have Christian parents. Those stable families that intentionally make church a focal point are to be considered a huge blessing to the children and to the church. In fact, 20 percent more students stay in churches where parents are authentic in their faith.[10]

A recent Associated Press poll revealed the importance of the parent connection. Spending time with family was rated as the top answer to an open-ended survey in which thirteen- to twenty-four-year-olds were asked what makes them happy.[11] The old excuse that teens and young adults just aren't interested in church, or that they are simply rebelling against their parents, doesn't hold water. Though teens may express outwardly a resistance to family time or going to church, inwardly they crave the stability and love that a family and local body of believers bring.

The goal is to be authentic. One of the reasons I (Sam) didn't stray from the church or rebel too much from my family was that my mother and father never crammed church down my throat, yet they still expected me to attend with the family. The balance is a tough one to make, but they managed to keep that balance most of the time. Additionally, my dad was a pastor, but he was the same person at home as he was at church. While tempers get lost and family members annoy one another, I knew that both he and my mom didn't put on a church face every Sunday and Wednesday. They were open, honest, and sincere with their struggles. They encouraged their three sons to act the same, following their example. I never felt the pressure to be the perfect pastor's kid; rather, my parents allowed me the freedom to develop my own personality and sense of self-awareness.

Now that I am a pastor, on occasion I will step into the pulpit and tell my church that I lost my temper in a road rage fit or that my morning didn't go exactly as planned. A church is not the assembly of perfect people; church is the assembly of authentic people worshipping a perfect Savior. Parents in an essential church lay it all on the Lord's altar. Their children see their example. Though life may not be perfect, though the world may throw some nasty curveballs, parents in an essential church lovingly guide and discipline their children to be active participants in their church without playing the "perfect church life" game.

The essential church and the essential gospel. When a drought hits a region of the country, crops don't grow and yards get crispy fried. Everything gets dusty and dry except for the few areas where the water remains—beside the dripping faucet, up against the house where the sun doesn't hit, and along the creek. The grass doesn't grow for weeks on end and is beyond brown, an eerie color that makes for conspicuous stripes in rural backyards where lateral lines crisscross in septic systems.

The signs of a more intense drought are occurring in our great country. It has been going for some time; it is a drought in our churches. This drought stretches from coast to coast. With many people—particularly young adults—leaving the church every week, the church needs to get back to the basics.

We must pray for a pouring out of the Holy Spirit. Our society needs water, but it has abandoned the fountain of living water and dug cisterns for itself—a double evil because the Lord is abandoned and people resort to their own pursuits (see Jer. 2:13). The powers of darkness are bringing the heat and causing extreme spiritual droughts.

But a fountain of living water is available from a well that quenches eternally the dryness of desiccated, sinful flesh. Our anhydrous lives can become soaked in the pouring out of the Holy Spirit. The damage brought by the drought can be reversed. Planted seeds dormant in dusty soil can germinate in the true light.

The church needs sowers, pray-ers, and warriors. Churches need people unafraid of gospel boldness. Churches need pastors willing to live out an evangelistic fervor, modeling a soul-winning attitude for their congregation. Churches need a body of believers unafraid to ask the Holy Spirit to wake up their community. Churches need natural, God-given unity in denominational politics, not a coerced and forced uniformity. Churches need accountability in all aspects of our Christian lives. We need a fresh crop of humble seminarians willing to take the country churches of six and lead them to become the country churches of twenty-five. Churches need a renewed focus on the total reliance of our sovereign God. Churches need a throng of Christians willing to lay down their lives for their fellow brothers and sisters. Churches need more backyard missionaries. We need more multicultural churches, and we need churches that are essential to the lives of their people.

CHAPTER 2

Looking for a Different Kind of Community

The annual event Thunder over Louisville was an instant hit when it started in the early 1990s and draws all types of people from the local community. "Thunder," as the locals call it, kicks off the two-week-long Derby Festival, which leads up to the Kentucky Derby on the first Saturday in May. Thunder occurs two weeks prior to the Derby on a Saturday. The April weather in Louisville can range from snowy to sunny, perfect days. But nothing keeps the throngs of people from venturing downtown to be Thunderstruck.

More than eight hundred thousand people journey to the grand banks of the Ohio River to witness the daylong air show that culminates in the largest fireworks display in North America. Tens of thousands of shells rocket from barges and bridges in one of the greatest pyrotechnic displays in the world.

Interstates are shut down due to the fireworks. Even I-65, a major north-south corridor in the eastern United States, is blocked for the duration of the thirty-minute show. The event has become so popular that prime riverfront spots are taken quickly. Some resort to camping in the park the night before to stake their claim on a precious piece of the great lawn on the riverfront. The sight is enough to make any Kentuckian proud— almost a million people all chanting in unison the countdown for the fireworks to begin.

Thirty minutes later, it's over.

Then everyone starts fighting one another to get back to their cars.

Then road rage replaces the gleeful unity of the people of Louisville.

The police officers do all they can, but the traffic jams last for hours as one million people all try to turn the same direction on the same interstate.

It reminds us of the noon Sunday rush hour.

Somewhere along the way "church" for some people became a once-a-week event, an event with no sense of community. It is ironic that the church, which is supposed to be the locus of community, does not provide a sense of community for many of the dechurched. And as a consequence, these young people move to different places to connect with others. They are looking for a different kind of community. This generation desires an essential connection with others.

Won't You Be My Neighbor?

Where did this sense of community go? How did the church community become nonessential? And how can the church reclaim the bond? The problem is not new. We read in the book of Hebrews that some were habitually neglecting the fellowship (Heb. 10:25). The issue of church dropouts is obviously not a new phenomenon.

The subject of community goes much deeper. It is more than just a weekly gathering. It goes beyond the walls of the church. You can't create community by spiritual navel-gazing. Nor does building a gym create community. Even adding a few candles won't solve the problem.

Churches that become the locus of community have it built into their DNA. It isn't their programs, buildings, or style. The people of the church create community.

Reaching your neighbors requires you to surrender time and convenience. Jesus understood what it was like to experience the coming and going of people. Mark 6:30–44 reveals that after an exhausting day Jesus attempts to escape the massive crowd, retreating by boat. But the crowd follows Him on foot, beating Him and the disciples to the next destination. Instead of venting frustration and starting off to yet another place, Jesus has deep compassion for the people.

He decides that a meal is in order for everyone.

Then He tells the disciples to feed them.

They calculate the cost of the meal and spin their heads over how to accomplish this task.

This task is impossible. They are in the middle of the desert. More than five thousand people are hungry, waiting to be fed both physically and spiritually. The disciples don't have the money to purchase food, and even if they did, there is no place to buy it. All they can scrounge up is five small rolls and two dried fish.

Jesus looks up to heaven, appealing to God for the miraculous. The impossible becomes reality through the power of God. Two fish and five rolls multiply. Kingdom resources don't run out. Everyone was satisfied. Many who were poor probably had a full belly for the first time in their lives.

This was not only a time of sharing food. People from many different communities and backgrounds interacted. Most of the surrounding towns had fewer than three thousand people. This gathering of five thousand plus would have been much larger than most had ever seen. The miracle of food multiplying isn't the only important piece of the story. Also important are the conversations that occurred after the meal in small groups of people discussing Jesus and His teaching.

The sheep without a shepherd now had guidance. The aimless groups of people were being shaped by the words of hope. They were filled spiritually and physically. The Source of living water, the Bread of life, met the needs of this hodgepodge assemblage of people. He did so at the sacrifice of much-desired rest. Jesus surrendered time and convenience in order to reach a group of people searching for a sense of community.

I (Sam) loathe inefficiencies. I detest giving up my time. I know every function of Microsoft Outlook. I've been known to plan vacations in spreadsheets in fifteen-minute increments, including travel destinations and mile marker ETAs. (Note: I am not speaking in hyperbole. I have actually done this before.) My family says I take planning to an extreme. But I say, "What's more fun than planning all the fun that you plan on having?" Admittedly I am by nature an overplanner. I focus on efficiency to the point of inefficiency.

Our time is valuable, and few value it more than I. But a considerable part of the problem with creating community in the church is the grand issue of time. At no time in my life did I realize this more than right before my wedding.

One day a couple of weeks before we were married, my future wife began to move some of her belongings into my townhouse. As we were pulling out of the driveway that day, she commented, "Oh, and I can't wait to meet your neighbors!"

I sat silent. She gave me her frustrated face. I tried not to look back.

"You don't know your neighbors yet?!"

"No," I said with a twinge of guilt.

"You've lived here almost four years, and you haven't even said hello to your neighbors?"

"I'm busy. Besides, they don't want to be disturbed either," I said meekly.

"Honey," she said graciously, "you *should* know your neighbors."

Erin and I have different backgrounds. She grew up in the same small town her entire life. She lived in two different houses, yet both were on the same street. I moved about every two to four years to different states. She has deep roots. I never planted them. She knows everyone in her town, and we cannot go anywhere without someone coming up to us and saying hello. She once had a ten-minute conversation with the teller at the bank through the drive-through microphone. I never even gave a thought to knowing the person who lives across the street, let alone the teller at my bank.

In Luke 10, a lawyer questions Christ, asking what he must do to inherit eternal life. The answer: he must love God with his entire being. Christ then adds that he must love his neighbor as himself.

The lawyer retorts, to save face after his trick question backfired, "And who is my neighbor?"

Christ responds with one of the most popular parables in the Bible, the Good Samaritan. A priest and a Levite, religious figures in the community, passed by a man in need. The Samaritan, an outcast in their society, came to the man's rescue. The Samaritan was the good neighbor.

Our society has become increasingly mobile, and people are moving to different towns with greater frequency over further distances. The *Wall Street Journal* reported in October 2006 that people drive 79 percent more miles than they did in 1982 while roadways have only increased 3 percent, creating a frustrated commuter society living in permanent gridlock.[1] People get home late in the evening, open their garage, and go right inside. Getting to know your neighbors has almost become a hassle.

Despite my own frustration in this area, I believe my wife is correct (of course). We *should* know our neighbors. We may have to schedule time with them, take the initiative, or simply make an effort to say hello. Christ calls us to be good neighbors. And this call extends beyond our own subdivisions, condos, and apartments. It is a call to the world. Our neighbors will never see Christ exemplified in our lives unless we show them.

Sociologically, the subject of community is amorphous. Within a community a group of people share an environment with common beliefs, intent, resources, preferences, needs, and risks.[2] The church community can feel unshaped just like the culture around it. But there is something that gives the church community definition, structure, and glue.

Jesus is the glue. His Word gives our churches structure.

Jesus Christ holds the members of the body together. He shapes the community of the church. He is the head. He gives a local congregation form. When the body attempts to usurp the role of the head, the bond loosens. The issue of church community gets down to the DNA level. The essential connection of community must revolve around relationships focused on Christ. He is the bond and the glue.

> ### Essentially This
>
> The most outwardly focused churches are many times the healthiest on the inside.

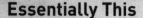

Changing the atmosphere of the church is just not enough. Changing the setting or the physical features of the church won't solve the problem.

The people of the church must make a conscious decision to stop looking inwardly and begin to reach outwardly. An inwardly focused church community is a dying community because they are letting go of the bond that holds them together.

A vital church community centers on the message of Jesus Christ and the going and telling of that message to those in the community outside of the church. In other words, an essential church community is a sacrificial church community that surrenders time and convenience for the sake of telling others about Jesus Christ. Get people fired up about the Great Commission and watch a strong church community unfold.

This mode of thinking is counterintuitive, but it's true: a missional church thinking outwardly is a healthy church inwardly. When churches begin to focus on how to reach the community instead of spending all their time on existing programs and people, the current people of the church grow stronger. Totally neglecting the current ministries, people, and programs is not the point. Rather, by shifting the focus of these ministries and people outward, the existing relationships among people are strengthened. When the people of the church proclaim the message of Jesus to the world, the glue of the church community holds the members more tightly to one another.

Putting an Age on the Exodus

The younger generation is looking for a different kind of community. But at what age does this search result in action? And what is the critical point at which this generation realizes that their current community is not something to which they feel they belong? In the introduction we detailed the flash point at which teens begin leaving the church. The sweet sixteen birthday is not so sweet for the church. The church begins losing teens instead of gaining teens at the age of sixteen. The net gain of previous ages starts to become a net loss at around age sixteen for most congregations. The exodus from the church community picks up steam from age seventeen forward, and it becomes a flood when teens hit the ripe old age of twenty.

The next chart demonstrates the widening gap between those teens attending church at least twice a month and those who do not. As it reveals, the largest spread between dropouts and those who stay occurs at age twenty.

Twice-a-month church attendance by age[3]		
	Dropouts	**Those who stay**
Age 16	65%	74%
Age 17	51%	71%
Age 18	29%	72%
Age 19	14%	63%
Age 20	12%	65%
Age 21	13%	64%
Age 22	13%	62%

As the chart illustrates, half of all dropouts are still attending church at least twice a month at age seventeen. This attendance begins to decline steeply at age eighteen, with only 29 percent of all dropouts still attending church. By age twenty the spread between dropouts and those who stay is at its largest. After age twenty the spread between the dropout rate and the rate of those that stay begins to plateau.

We cannot underscore enough the gravity of reaching, relating, engaging, and assimilating teens in the church. Even though they may be immature, moody, and possibly a bit rebellious, the church should not relegate them to spiritual corners. Leaders in the church cannot neglect the care of this younger generation. The best time to assimilate them into the community is the time in their lives when they are the most distant and hardest to engage. The church community must work harder at meeting these teens where they are, lest they lose them to another community outside the church forever.

Autumn's Story

What if the surrounding community is not like the people of the church? What if the church culture and the culture of the community don't exactly match? How does the church community reach a community outside? How does a church create a different kind of community?

An essential church is a changing church because different types of people are always entering the community. An essential church has a different kind of community.

Autumn Davis understands this dynamic.[4] She is a missionary in Sheffield, England. To a twenty-four-year-old Texas native, England is a far cry from the culture and community in which she grew up. But she's there to minister to the youth of Sheffield and create a bond between her church and those on the outside.

Autumn pointed to Ezekiel 37, where God asked the prophet a pivotal question as he stared at the valley of dry bones: "Can these bones live?"

Believing that God has the power to resurrect, Ezekiel prophesied as he had been commanded. Then "the breath entered them, and they came to life and stood on their feet, a vast army."

"You see bones? I see an army!" Autumn exclaimed.

Autumn believes an army is emerging in Sheffield, England—an army of young people who will lay down their lives for the cause of Christ. She longs to see this army come to life. She longs for a revival of teens and young adults in England.

Autumn noticed the community of skaters that congregated at the skate park just across the street from her church. They wore black. They had piercings in every body part imaginable. She saw a different community, an outcast community. They were not the nice, prepackaged families of five that the church typically draws. But she took her church community to them. She met them where they were—at the skate park.

She brought free sodas and pizza. Autumn bought a skate-board. She had never skateboarded, but she started to learn. This young Texan became respected and loved among the youth of Sheffield. She took art supplies with her and engrained herself more in the street culture. She painted with them. She asked them to paint how they see God. She and her church performed street dramas around the local hangouts. She conversed. She reached outward.

They played capture the flag in the local parks. Autumn makes the point that capture the flag also means a captive audience. Play the game, and then share the gospel of Jesus. They held an art camp called RE:Create. They put on skate competitions.

Then Autumn invited them to a small group at her house. She shared the gospel message of Jesus Christ. More students started coming. More students started hanging out with Autumn and her different kind of community. These youth began coming to The Gathering, the worship service for her church. Worship at this church is different from the average Sunday service around the United States. But the message is the same: "I am the way, the truth, and the life. No one comes to the Father except through Me" (John 14:6).

Then it happened. Courtney, one of the students, decided to follow Jesus. She saw the light in Autumn. Courtney heard the knocking. She opened the door, and Jesus came into her life. Courtney became a child of God. She entered into the community of believers in Sheffield, England.

She stood in front of the church the day she accepted Christ and told the congregation, "I'm free. For the first time in my life, I'm free."

One church in England. One Texan named Autumn. And a different type of community. They all came together with the glue of the church. The eternal link of Jesus bonded them together as only the grace of God can accomplish. May the dry bones of England live!

The Goldilocks Dilemma

Autumn maintained a balance with this new community of youth that she wanted to reach. She did not get so close to these teenagers that she became part of their community, participating in some of their illicit activities. But she was not so distant that they looked at her as a religious outsider. Striking this balance is tough; we dub it the Goldilocks Dilemma.

Churches should relate to and serve their communities so that people will come to know Christ. The conundrum, however, is to engage the culture without compromising our call as Christians to be set apart. And that is the crux of it all: how do you get it just right? As in the story of Goldilocks, where hot or cold porridge doesn't pass muster, the church must be neither too hot nor too cold to culture. Too hot and you become the culture from which Christians are set apart. Too cold and you become an island reaching no one.

Many reading this section will immediately conjure images of what one of our friends in ministry calls "the church for cool people." Several new descriptive buzzwords are popping up all over church Web sites—*relevant, engaging,* and *conversational* to name a few. We use them too. But you don't have to be trendy to engage the community of people around you. Nor do you need to know everything about their culture to carry on a conversation with them. But you do need to love them. And you do need to be genuinely interested in what they have to say. New taglines alone do not help; a heart for the lost is the key.

This problem of balancing the seesaw of reaching the community without compromising the truth is pervasive. One survey states that only half of churches feel that they do a good job of engaging the community and making others feel welcome. Additionally, only 40 percent of these churches feel that they have any real impact on the community or the world.[5] This survey was taken among people within the church. So 60 percent of the people in our churches do not believe they are making an impact in their community. If you were to ask the people outside of these churches, the statistics would probably be much worse.

In order to see firsthand how this balance is maintained, we visited a church in a downtown Midwestern city that exemplifies this passion for the lost. The church would not be considered traditional or typical. It's probably one of those "churches for cool people." We wouldn't know. But we were surprised by the church and had the opportunity to meet with one of the founding lay leaders.

In order to have a place to worship, the congregation recently renovated an old three-story elementary school. Since the church is located on a one-way street, parking was a snap. When we walked into the main area, we were greeted and handed cups of coffee (from a local shop). The first thing we noticed was the beautiful hardwood floors and art exhibits in the main congregating area. We were surprised by the number of people there early, as well as their diversity. We were in the minority since neither of us has yet obtained our first tattoo. No one seemed to care, though, and the atmosphere in the room was welcoming.

The church has two main services on Sunday, one in the morning and one in the evening. Combined, they now have about five hundred to six hundred attending in a given week. They started in a house a few years back. The service was more liturgical than what we were used to, but the message from the pastor (who wore an untucked shirt and jeans) was expository. He was one year into a two-year sermon series through Matthew. And he certainly didn't compromise the gospel in any way. We could see this church wasn't concerned with being cool. They were just reaching a forgotten community in the city for Christ.

This church had managed to balance reaching and serving their community while still proclaiming the timeless gospel message. Clearly, a church in an urban setting will have a different community than a church in one of the surrounding rural counties.

And each of these churches will have to engage their respective communities in differing fashions. This church was a Goldilocks church.

Our culture today needs more of them. We are called to be salt and light. Salt adds flavor, and light illuminates the darkness. We are to be the spice of culture yet also shine to the truth of Jesus Christ. How is all this done? There certainly is no single all-encompassing cookie-cutter answer for every church.

We went to dinner with the church lay leader and discussed these points over a hot bowl of gumbo in a local joint down the road from the church. We came to the conclusion that churches like his are hard to define, but you know it when you see it. By the way, the gumbo was just right, spicy enough for a kick but not enough to give you indigestion.

Disenchantment with the Status Quo

Disenchantment with the status quo exists. Many churches are mired in unnecessary traditions, irrelevant rules and regulations, and a culture of the past. Drive through many towns, and at the heart of the community is a church that once was the center of activity. Community energy once emanated from inside it, but now the building sits dormant throughout much of the week.

Many people claim a church. You meet people in the community, strike up a conversation, and you ask, "Do you have a church home?"

"Oh, yes, we go to . . ."

You are glad to hear they have found a connection and

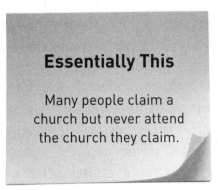

Essentially This

Many people claim a church but never attend the church they claim.

continue with the rest of the conversation, now avoiding any talk of inviting them to your church because you don't believe in pulling people from other churches.

In reality they are CEOs. They *claim* a particular church, but they *attend* church only on Christmas, Easter, and Other special events.

The spread between those who claim a church and those who actually attend on any given week is substantial.

In a Rainer Research survey, we found that only 28 percent of the United States population stated they attended a Protestant church in a given week. Yet the *CIA World Factbook* states that 52 percent of the United States population claims they are Protestant. By extrapolating this data to national population figures, we can estimate the size of this disenchanted population. Our conclusion is that as many as 73.3 million self-professing Protestants on a national scale may be unconnected to a church. Clearly the number is larger when Catholics and other groups are considered.[6]

We certainly do not claim to have pinned down the exact number of disenchanted church people in the United States. But what is overwhelming about these estimates is the sheer size of the spread between those who claim a church and those who attend. As a result, we can say unequivocally that this issue of community is highly relevant indeed.

Our conclusion: many people who claim a church (or at least Protestantism) are not attending a church! They associate with the concept of church, yet they don't go. People are not leaving their religious beliefs behind; they just step away from the local body. Our nation is full of people seeking religious connections, but they are not connecting with the church.

To be blunt, church is superfluous to them.

Seventy-three million people give evidence of inadequate churches.

Tens of millions are unable to find community with a local body.

Our nation cries out for essential churches.

Church Swappers and the Madness of Crowds

In Mark 3:7–12 Jesus ministered to a large mass of people. This crowd followed Him not because they were seeking the Messiah. Rather, they sought a miracle-worker. With so many trying to touch Christ, a religious frenzy of pushing and shoving resulted.

Christ was forced to retreat by boat and then camp on a mountain to avoid the throngs of people. It was against this backdrop that the twelve apostles were chosen, an intimate group of loyal (though sometimes immature) men who would eventually carry the gospel message of Jesus into a lost world.

In this short passage is a picture of human behavior. We tend to flock toward popularity without regard for legitimacy. While Christ is the great Savior of the world, most of the crowd in this passage (like people today) were there simply because He was the popular new healer of the hour.

In his classic *Extraordinary Popular Delusions and the Madness of Crowds*, Charles MacKay wrote about specific historical events in which human folly ousted normal reason in the pursuit of mass hysteria. His thesis: people are easily swayed by public manipulation and the latest waves of appeal.[7]

The best-known historical case of this mob mentality occurred in the Netherlands in the 1600s. People went crazy over tulips. In fact, some paid as much as ten times the average yearly income for one tulip bulb; huge mansions were cheaper than one flower! In 1637 the tulip bubble burst, and prices plummeted back to normal. But the aftermath was not pretty; hoards of people were left with nothing.

Many of our churches experience their own form of tulip mania: swarms of churchgoers gravitate toward the church they think is the most popular or best suited for their needs. We will admit that this phenomenon does occur at times. And many of these churches have superb pastoral leadership and are fully obedient to the Great Commission. They are megachurches because they truly want the lost saved and the body discipled. Their church is healthy and, as a result, large. But other churches are simply drawing a crowd.

Does this church-swapper description best describe the youngest generation of dropouts? Are they falling prey to the madness of church crowds? Are they leaving their community for a bigger, better community where the rest of the crowd has swung?

Our research reveals a different tale.

Frequent church switchers are not a major problem with the dropout generation. The chart below demonstrates that both dropouts and those who stay seek about the same number of

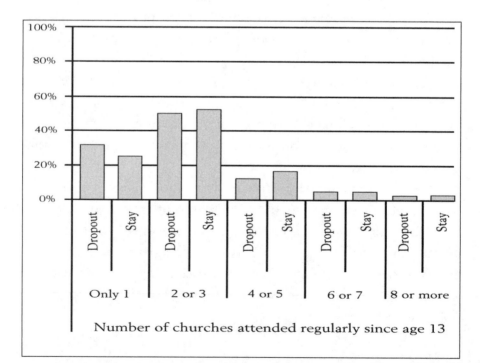

church communities. After two or three different communities, these teens either settle on a church or drop out for good.

Church-swapping is not a major problem with this generation. While many students likely attend church with their parents, these families are not skipping from local church to local church. The vast majority of dropouts attend two or three churches. Additionally, the vast majority of those that stay in the church are not hopping congregations. In fact, the difference between church dropouts and those that stay is minimal. Neither group is guilty of much church-switching. This generation is not jumping to several churches over the course of their young adult period of life. While many decry the massive herding of believers from one church to another (and rightly so), this phenomenon does not occur predominantly in the younger generation. They either find an essential community and stay, or they leave what they perceive as the nonessential church for good.

Where Is the Third Place?

What happened? How did so many churches lose ground as the locus of community? The church lost its place as a community gathering point. Once the center of connection, the church became an ancillary part of the greater community.

We want the church to regain its status as the "third place." This answer is not a panacea for churches, but it is a piece of the equation.

So what is a third place? And how do churches become one?

The "third place" term was coined by sociologist Ray Oldenburg. The concept of a third place involves a gathering place for people separate from home (the first place) and work (the second place). The third place is an anchor of the community, which facilitates relational interaction between people in the community.[8] These informal meeting places have existed throughout history, but they have increased in importance the last decade. As the lines between home and work blur due to the increasing mobility of society and as people travel a greater distance from home to work, the third place has become an important gathering point for people wanting to break between the first and second place.

A major difference between the latest generation and older generations is that the younger crowd intentionally seeks these places for entertainment. The third place is marketed to them as something worthwhile. In fact, millions of people pay to experience the sensation of the third place. That's why a Starbucks is found on so many street corners. It's a dollar cup of coffee combined with a three-dollar experience of communal gathering. In fact, many meetings between the two authors occurred in Starbucks during the writing of this book. (Sam prefers the vanilla latte; Thom savors the caramel macchiato.)

We believe the church must reclaim the status of the third place.

Indeed, essential churches already grasp this concept. Through our research we found that churches who are reaching the unchurched and dechurched understand this trend of creating community. Most of them offer a third place in their churches. While only one out of five churches with recent facility additions built a third-place facility, almost three-fourths of the formerly unchurched say they were attracted to a church with a third-place facility.[9]

Let us be clear: building a coffee shop in your church is *not* the magic bullet, but healthy churches that have third-place facilities are more likely to attract the unchurched, particularly those in the eighteen to twenty-two age range. These churches are more likely to see the dechurched become rechurched.

The ambiance of the third place is a critical component of an essential church, but it is *secondary*. The unchurched and dechurched are *primarily* motivated to go to church due to a feeling of void in their lives and the simple fact that someone invited them.[10] Therefore, while they are not a solution in themselves, third-place facilities help an essential church attract the unchurched.

Additionally, our research uncovered the gym fallacy. Many pastors hear from their members that building a gym will help attract the unchurched in their community. We, however, found the exact opposite to be true. In fact, one of the areas of the church that was least important to the unchurched was the gym. Church leaders who are considering building gyms need to understand that gyms in general serve their current membership and have little effect on attracting the unchurched or with creating an atmosphere of the third place.

The Tired Battle over Worship Style

Essential churches come in all shapes and sizes and . . . styles. Gasp! Hard to believe, we know. Surprisingly, the vast majority of dropouts did not leave because of a preference over worship style. Only 10 percent of dropouts mentioned one of the reasons for their departure from church was because the worship style was unappealing to them.[11]

Q: "So worship style has little to do with people leaving the church?"

A: "Correct."

Q: "You mean to tell me that we aren't losing people because of our style?"

A: "Yes."

Q: "Even our students and young adults?"

A: "Yup."

Q: "Style isn't the reason for lack of community?"

A: "Nope."

Q: "So we can't place the blame for the exodus of people from our church on style?"

A: "No."

The battle over worship style is tired. Shall we let it rest? Of all the reasons people told us they left the church, style was not in the top ten. In fact, it wasn't even in the top twenty-five. The issue of style is important for the conversation concerning contextualization of worship, but it is not a critical reason that students eighteen to twenty-two leave your church.

Students don't drop out of church because an organ toots instead of a guitar screeching. They drop out because their church is not essential to them. They may gripe at times over worship style, but most of them aren't prepared to leave the church over the issue.

We talked with one young couple who worship in a traditional church (though they call themselves blended).

"Is style an issue for you?"

"Somewhat," replied the husband, "I personally prefer a more upbeat service over what we have currently."

"Is it a major sticking point for you?"

"Not so much."

"So you wouldn't leave the church if you were told they would never change the style?"

"No, I don't think so."

"Why?" we asked.

"I grew up here. The church has been through ups and downs. I've had peaks and valleys in my life too, but the people were always here for me. I want to be here for them too. I'd leave for more important reasons if it came down to it but not the style of worship."

Worship style is a much-debated issue. Some handle the conversation with love, only wanting to worship God appropriately. Others get red-faced at the sound of anything other than their end of the musical spectrum. The issue does carry some weight, but it has little to do with people leaving the church.

Young adults leave because they lose a connection to the community of believers. Style of worship plays a small part in the creation of this community. In other words, it's not the music. Rather, the people of the church make meaningful relationships, a sense of connection, and a comfortable place to gather.

Loitering Allowed

Not all dropouts leave for good. Many continue to hang around the church, coming on occasion. About one-third of dropouts age twenty-three to thirty continue to come to church once a month or less.[12] They do not remain active, but they loiter in the church.

These loiterers go under the radar. They don't fill out guest cards because they know they are technically part of the church. Church members are likely to ignore them because of perceived tension. Active members think they dropped out because something was wrong. The loiterer thinks the members will look down on them if they try to return full-time.

Most of the time these young adults feel guilty about their neglect of the fellowship. Before the silence of active members prompts them to depart permanently, churches should reach out to this group of hangers-on. Surprisingly, it may take only one conversation to make a person feel "rewelcomed." Many already maintain a sense of inward guilt. A firm yet loving conversation could be the impetus behind the church reclaiming them. Instead of loitering as a perceived outcast, they will let out a sigh of relief once they learn that the church truly desires them to be back in the fold.

While we believe membership still matters, don't put up figurative "no loitering" signs. Tear them down by reaching out to the irregular attenders. Let them know that the expectations are high for members, but also inform them that the church would want nothing more than for them to return. The best growth in a church is always conversion growth, people coming to know Jesus as their personal Lord and Savior and being baptized in the church. The second best type of growth, however, is growth by absent members returning to the church. If the spread between your church roles and church attendance looks like Pac-Man in an Excel chart, examine the list of inactive people for those who might come back if simply invited. The response might prove more positive than you think.

Spiritual Refrigerators

If you are a night owl, then you probably have experienced the fourth meal. Hunger pains are not yet striking, but the glow of the refrigerator light beckons. Crossing the cold kitchen floor, you open the door and stare, looking for nothing in particular. We are all guilty, and we've all wolfed down a bologna sandwich or two at one in the morning. OK, so maybe not all of us.

Churches are like spiritual refrigerators for people. The curious will come and open the door. They stare inside. Many are not looking for anything specific. They may visit on occasion and then leave. Many church dropouts fall into this category. They are opening the doors of our places of worship and looking. They're looking for something, but they don't know what it is.

A sense of community is a strong pull for those who are searching, whether they have departed from the church or never stepped foot in a church. While this connection with the church is intangible, we uncovered through our research that encouragement is a significant tool. Indeed, half of the dropouts who return do so because of encouragement from either family or friends.[13]

Students like to search; they like the journey. But they aren't necessarily seeking to find. They want to connect with God, but they don't use spiritual tools to make this connection. The community of the church can help provide the encouragement for them to make the connection.

The potential for a great harvest is evident; we know the younger generation is searching. At their core they understand that a void exists in their lives. Otherwise, they would not search.

They are a receptive group. And with the right tone and delivery, they will listen to what the church has to say.

Many are just looking in spiritual refrigerators. They don't know what they want. They may not even be hungry for the Word, but at least they're looking. It is the church's responsibility to show them exactly what they need—the Bread of Life and Living Water. Essential churches create an essential community where the essential truth of Jesus is experienced.

This community is one where hard-to-love people are loved. It's one where unity in diversity is found. It's a community where people learn to engage a world yearning for truth. It's one where scarlet sins are washed white as snow. It's an inclusive community where the exclusive gospel is proclaimed. It's a community where people think outwardly instead of inwardly. It's a different kind of community, but it's one where Jesus lives.

CHAPTER 3

That's Life!
It Changes

W hen I transferred to a different college, things just changed."

Jeannette was a waitress at a local sports grill. We met with her after her shift late one evening to discuss her involvement in the local church. Cheery and smiling, she was gracious enough to answer our questions openly and honestly. She was still in her work clothes, but it didn't seem to bother her as we conversed in one of the vacant booths in the restaurant.

"Neither of my parents were Christians, so it didn't bother them one way or the other whether I was in church growing up. We would go as a family on Christmas and Easter and sometimes for a special event. But church was obviously not an important aspect of any of my family members' lives."

"Do you still attend a local church?" we asked.

"Not really. I go every now and then to the large church up the road about five miles, but I haven't been in a while."

"So what happened when you transferred colleges?"

"In all honesty, the major change in my life was my circle of friends."

"Did this help or hinder your connection to a church?"

Jeannette took a big sigh but kept her smiling demeanor.

"At my first school I had a group of friends who were Christians. They were always leading something at the church. A couple of them felt like they were called into the ministry. So they would use their spring break to go on a mission trip to some country where people needed help. Or they would spend their weekends helping out with a major event at the church. They were always highly involved in the church. Since that's where they hung out, I would hang out with them there."

"But when your group of friends changed with the transfer, you didn't find another circle of friends with the same level of involvement?"

Jeannette raised both eyebrows, smiled, and shook her head. "You nailed it."

We paused for a sip of coffee, and she interjected, "Wait, I can't blame my lack of church involvement on a circle of friends. It's my fault."

"How do you feel it's your fault?"

She stared at the wall several moments. We could tell she was choosing her words carefully.

"Do you know what I want to do with my life?" she asked rhetorically. "I want to help people as a nurse. That's why I transferred schools—to get into a good nursing program. I've never been one to plant roots; I just go. And since I'm that way, I figured the best thing for me to do to better the world is to travel to developing countries and help those who don't have access to many modern medical necessities."

We both listened intently to Jeannette as she poured out to us her sense of calling.

"I have to admit, the best way for me to use my gifts is through the church. I want to go on missions trips. I would love to go to Africa and work with children. More than anything I just want to help people across the world, people that typically don't get what they need in life. I should be doing this through the church, and I'm not even attending a church!"

"What's the great barrier for you in finding a church that would enable you to fulfill your calling?"

Her passion was still evident. "First, I want to attend a church that actually goes on these types of trips. I've never been outside of the United States, so I don't know where to begin myself. If I really am called to do this full time, it would be great if I could begin small with some church trips. But I don't know of any churches around here that do these trips. Perhaps it's my fault for not asking."

"Jeannette, we know of a church in this area that participates in missions. We can certainly get you connected with them."

She started smiling again.

Jeannette's story is not typical, but the catalyst for her departure from the church is typical. A change in life prompts a church departure. A common story among the dechurched is that the life change that comes with adulthood made them reevaluate all the networks in their lives.

Jeannette's network of people shifted when her life made a turn in a different direction. Though dropping out of the church was admittedly her own fault, she lost her one connection to the church—her friends. This change caused her to rethink her priorities, and church became less of a priority in her life.

She desired this change. It was a change that she sought. It was a good change for her. She was happy with the change. She wanted to be a nurse so she transferred schools to accomplish this goal. This type of change occurs frequently in life. Sam and Thom have both experienced it. You probably have as well. You reach a goal in life and set another goal. The job offer for which you've been working finally becomes available. Your spouse changes careers and uproots the family to a different location. You go away to college. You have a child. Or something tragic happens that shuffles every priority in your life.

Active churchgoers across the nation can experience an infinite number of individual life changes. While some patterns of change exist, such as swarms of eighteen-year-olds going away to college the fall following their high school graduation, these changes are different for each person.

More than likely, you are familiar with the television show *Survivor*. And yes, the show is still on as of this writing. No, we don't watch it any more either. But the concept is simple. A group of people in a harsh environment play a game to see who can survive the longest in the climate around them. Each week someone new is voted off the island by the remaining group of people until one lone survivor wins the game. Real life plays out like this game in a similar fashion. We all have a set of priorities in life from which we must choose the most important. We choose priorities that are the most critical to our daily life. Many other secondary and tertiary priorities are neglected or tossed out. The problem is that the church is not one of the main priorities. The church is often "voted off the island" during the months and years of transition following a change.

Our research found that the vast majority of church dropouts indicated they dropped out of church because of a life change. Ninety-seven percent of dropouts stated that one reason they left the church was a change in their lives. Of all the major categories prompting someone to leave the church, this life-change category was by far the most influential.

Do you remember the top ten life changes that affect the younger generation's church attendance? Some of them surprised us. They might surprise you as well.

Top Ten Life Changes That Cause People to Drop Out of Church

1. Simply wanted a break from church
2. Moved to college
3. Change in work responsibilities
4. Moved too far away from church
5. Became too busy, though still wanted to attend
6. Spending more time with friends outside of church
7. School responsibilities preventing me from attending church
8. Wanted to make life decisions not accepted by the church
9. Family and/or home responsibilities preventing me from attending
10. Lost touch with my churchgoing friends

Many of the above changes sound almost mundane. People move into bigger houses. They move closer to a better school for their children. They change shifts at their job. They get inundated with a project at work that pulls them away for an extra fifteen hours a week. They lose touch with a couple of friends who were the reason they attended a particular church. Grandma moves into the basement. The kids go to college at the university two hours from home. Sunday becomes the only day to sleep in because of ultrabusy American life. Typical change. Normal change. Change that everyone experiences at some point.

The talking heads talk a lot about change.

Change the church. Rethink the way church should be done. Reinvent church.

We admit that much needs to change with the church. As discussed in the introduction, the American church is in a rapid state of decline. But another realm of change is occurring. This change is outside the church, not inside. The people of the church are experiencing changing lives from forces outside of the fellowship. They have pressures other than the church that are pulling them in myriad directions. Many of your fellow brothers and sisters in Christ are feeling the burden of change. Sometimes this change is good. Sometimes it is what people want. Sometimes it is mundane. Other times change is unexpected and tragic.

Essential churches cope with changes inside the church and outside the church. An essential church not only pushes to improve internal ministries; it also gears these ministries to accommodate for the change that the people of the church experience from their daily lives. These churches understand the dynamics of life changes.

Life happens.

Change occurs.

Change itself becomes the catalyst, and many times this change prompts a departure from the local church fellowship.

Busyness and Bolting

We're busy people. We bolt about our daily routine in a tornado of rapid activity. Time is a precious commodity, and we fill our time with as many activities as possible. We cram one-hour tasks into fifteen minutes, and then we speed twenty-five miles over the speed limit to make up for the rest. We overcommit. We underplan. We procrastinate. We're perpetually late. Then we complain about little sleep and no time for exercise or leisure. Americans spend their time like their money, using as much as they have (if not more) and saving none. The Bureau of Labor Statistics reports that the average workday for people ages twenty-five to fifty-four consists of 7.6 hours of sleep, 8.2 hours of work, 2.6 hours of leisure and sports, 1 hour of household activities, 1.1 hours of eating and drinking, 1.1 hours of caring for others, and 2.4 other hours.[1] We don't know about you, but the 7.6 hours of sleep sound nice!

Believe it or not, 65 percent of Americans report spending more time with their personal computers than their own spouses.[2] Without a doubt we all clock too many hours in Internet hinterland. Additionally, Americans now spend more than one hundred hours a year commuting to and from work,[3] and it's driving us mad. The road is full of rage these days.

These statistics probably do not come as a surprise to you. In fact you may be thinking, *Only one hundred hours commuting and 2.6 hours of leisure time? I wish I had it that good!* Reading this section probably only adds concrete stats to what you already experience in your daily life. We stay busy, and we have little time for anything extra.

Through our research we were not surprised to learn that new and busy schedules often moved the church to a lower priority among the dechurched. But we were fascinated to learn *why* the church fell to such a low rung on the ladder.

As we mentioned in the introduction, more than two-thirds of young churchgoing adults in America drop out of church between the ages of eighteen and twenty-two. The number one reason they cited for their departure: *I simply wanted a break from church.* This finding surprised us. Church for so many people has become a chore. Particularly with the younger generation, church is another time slot to fill. It is a check box on the weekly to-do list. The churches of the dropouts were not a place where they wanted to spend free time. It was the

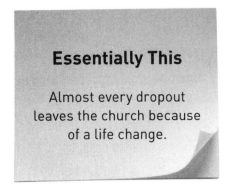

Essentially This

Almost every dropout leaves the church because of a life change.

opposite. Church was just another time waster for them. And 70 percent of young churchgoers decided that it was time to eliminate this segment of their life. Their church was not essential to them so it was one of the first items to come off the list when there was a time crunch.

As we mentioned earlier, the church and Christ are eternally tied. The two cannot be separated. The two are married to each other. Christ is the groom. The church is His bride. Trying to be a Christian without a connection to the local church is like trying to have a marriage without interacting and communicating with your spouse. The church is a critical piece of a relationship with God. In fact, a relationship with God is seriously compromised apart from the local church.

> For this reason a man will leave his father and mother
> and be joined to his wife, and the two will become one
> flesh. This mystery is profound, but I am talking about
> Christ and the church. (Eph. 5:31–32)

Christ and the church are bonded like the joining of a husband and wife in one flesh. Breaking this bond is serious. Yet droves of students are divorcing the church, and they do not cite irreconcilable differences. They do not leave mad. For many, no one compelling factor is pushing them away. They just want a little time off. They want their space. When they leave the church, there is no void. A gaping hole doesn't form when they exit. They leave quietly, and the church continues on as usual.

It Should Be Harder to Leave a Church Than to Join a Church

Now in his mid thirties, Brian had been absent from church for more than ten years . . . until recently. We sat with him in his small living room. Despite his large build and Marlboro Man appearance, he was somewhat shy and reserved. Talking slowly, deeply, and deliberately, he detailed for us why he was again active in a local church.

"My brother died about three months ago," he spoke softly, "and it shook me. He and I were close. It was a shock to my life."

"We're sorry to hear that, Brian."

He paused for several seconds and collected his train of thought.

"I wasn't living a horrible life. I was a good person for the most part. But I knew that God wanted more from me. I was not in a church, and I certainly wasn't worshipping Him in any way. But I didn't know where to turn."

"Was your previous church . . . ?"

We didn't finish our question before he interjected, "That church has lots of people I like in it, but I had not been there in several years. I left in my early twenties. At this point I don't even know why I left. I just decided one Sunday I wasn't going to go, and it soon became every Sunday."

He smiled tensely with his lips pressed tight, his moustache wrinkling, "It's almost humorous. They were so excited when I joined, threw a big party and all after I was baptized as a young man. But when I left, there was no concern from their end. They just kept on as usual. I was still a member up there, but I certainly didn't feel like it. I know it's my fault for leaving, but you would think there would be some level of accountability. I just never heard a thing from them."

He gave us another wry cowboy smirk. "It should be harder to leave a church than to join a church."

"Could you explain further what you mean by that?" We knew that he was hitting at the heart of the issue.

"When I came to know Jesus, I was just a rowdy young man. My brother and I weren't evil, but we did our fair share. Christ changed all that. I actually felt different after coming forward and talking with the pastor. I knew that God had given me a renewed outlook and purpose. But after I was baptized, the church didn't treat me any different than before I was saved. I wanted more, but I guess I just got bored with the same old stuff every Sunday."

He looked at his boots and continued, "Coming to Jesus is easy. The gospel message is simple. God accepts you as you are, and so should the church. My church accepted me. It was easy to come into the fellowship. While I take all the blame, I'm disappointed that they didn't make it hard for me to leave. Getting into a good church should be simple, but they should have such high expectations that it's impossible to leave. I just walked out the back door of my church without anyone batting an eye. I think most churches have it backwards. They make it difficult to get acquainted and a cakewalk to get unacquainted."

"Even after all that's happened between now and then, you do not doubt God?"

"Absolutely not." He was resolute. "Jesus Christ changed my life. Even though I've struggled with the death of my brother, I know God can get me through it."

"Tell us about your church that you've recently started attending."

"It started at the funeral. My old church sent flowers; my new church sent someone to talk with me."

"Did you think that was intrusive?"

"Not at all. The guy knew my parents from way back, and he just stopped by to say he was praying for me. He gave me his card and said to call him if I needed to."

"Obviously you took him up on his offer?"

"Yup, he offered to take me out for coffee. I'm not much for coffee shops, but I did invite him over here. And when he dropped by, he brought the pastor."

"What happened with that?" we had to ask.

"My pastor is a man of convictions. And he's not afraid of the truth. We didn't talk long before he told me, 'Brian, if you don't come to church on Sunday, I'm personally coming to this house and dragging you there by your nostrils.'"

Another wry smile. "I believed him. That Saturday night I actually pictured him coming to my house the following morning and pulling me to the worship service, pajamas and all."

We all laughed heartily. There's no way this moustache-man wore PJs.

Brian continued, "I know he doesn't deal with everyone that way, but it was what I needed to hear from a pastor. After working it out with my other church, I joined this church. And I don't see myself ever leaving."

Our time with Brian was revealing, encouraging, and caused us to think about the numerous churches we have consulted, attended, and pastored.

It should be harder to leave a church than join a church.

His words echoed in our ears.

The problem is at the DNA level of the church. Those churches that are prepared to disciple and help people like Brian have it built into their church culture. In other words, the entire atmosphere of the church is conducive to assimilation of young adults. Our research revealed that the atmosphere of the church has a measurable effect on those who leave, and it also is a predominant factor in keeping the younger generation within the church body.

Brian left the church in his early twenties. He was not exactly sure what prompted his departure. And no one aspect of his former fellowship is to blame. His church simply did not have an atmosphere that caused him to want to stay. So Brian took a break from church. As we stated earlier, this simple decision is the number one life change that causes the younger generation to leave.

No one issue pinpoints the driving factor for this decision to take a church sabbatical. There is no prevailing reason prompting this fellowship furlough. Most people will give you several unique and individual answers when questioned about their decision to take a break from their church, but our research uncovered some trends that linked the atmosphere of the church to the exodus of the gen X and gen Y people. In fact, the atmosphere of the church plays an appreciable role in either keeping or losing this generation. The following chart demonstrates the marked difference between churches with an atmosphere conducive for assimilation and those that do not have such an atmosphere.

What 18 to 22 year olds say about the atmosphere of their church[4]		
	Dropouts	Those who stay
Welcoming environment for my life stage	34%	72%
Other people like me attended	31%	67%
Offered appealing small-group studies for people in my life stage	29%	61%
Felt "at home"	27%	69%
Source of support during a personal crisis	26%	63%

Through this study we came to realize that the atmosphere, culture, and DNA of the church are critically important in preventing students from dropping out of church. Additionally, this same DNA is what helps a church become attractive to those on the outside. A stagnant atmosphere in the church makes it hard for the younger generation to breathe the spiritual air they are seeking. And stale environments make it easy for students to take a breather from church.

Welcome to our spiritual bastion! Churches that are welcoming to students tend to keep them. Unfortunately too often churches have large barriers to entry for college-age students. The front door is hard to squeeze through, but the back door is wide open.

If they do manage to break into the culture of the church, they do not stay for long. As evidenced in the previous chart, the church that provides a welcoming and applicable ministry for students at their relative life stage is better equipped to keep those students.

Most churches do not have a college and career ministry for young adults between the ages of eighteen and twenty-two. And the reason is not because these churches are located outside of college towns. Ten percent of the population in the United States is between the ages of eighteen and twenty-four.[5] That's more than thirty million student-age people! Even small towns have thousands of people in this age range. Do not blame your church's lack of a college ministry on the fact that you're not in a college town. The reality is not a dearth of students. The reality is that these students do not view the church as essential to their lives. The bond is broken. This younger generation has yet to realize the gravity of their relationship with the church. And the atmosphere of the church is not welcoming to them.

While churches should maintain ministries directed to people at different life stages, many youth ministries are too segregated.

They do their thing, and we'll do ours.

This train of thought is fundamentally flawed. The collective body of believers was designed to be integrated. Perhaps many youth leave because they see "their church" is over. It's finished. They no longer feel "at home" with others like themselves. They graduate from the high school ministry, and they don't flow into the "adult church" because it was never their church in the first place. Why transfer from a ministry that was directly relevant to them to another ministry that is geared for people decades older than them? So they take a break. They depart. And perhaps they think on their way out that they will return when they get a little older. When they match. When they fit in. When the "adult church" becomes germane to their stage in life.

With more than two-thirds of students eighteen to twenty-two dropping out of church, many of them simply because they wanted a break, we must begin to think about how to welcome people of all ages within the context of their life stage. Churches are not spiritual bastions for a select age group. Churches are not segregated entities between young and old. Rather, churches consist of a diverse body of believers at differing life stages, all working together in unity for the same purpose and goal of fulfilling the Great Commission.

Life happens. . . . Where's the church? Perhaps one of the most troubling findings with our research centered on what churches do for their people in times of personal crisis. Remember what Brian said?

It started at the funeral. My old church sent flowers; my new church sent someone to talk with me.

One of the major reasons Brian became active in a church again is because a congregation cared enough to pray for him during a difficult period in his life. As demonstrated in the previous chart on page 80, only 26 percent of dropouts stated that their church acted as a support network for them during a time of personal crisis. Conversely, 63 percent of those who stayed in their churches noted that the church had been a source of strength for them when they went through a critical stage of life.

If a church does not have a caring and compassionate atmosphere, it becomes difficult to keep students. A life crisis can be any number of things to a young adult. Leaving home, paying bills for the first time, the increased workload of new studies, getting involved in a serious relationship, among many other things, can all add up to a stressful stage of life. The church that maintains the disconnected attitude of *it builds character—I had to do it too and survived, so you'll be fine* will most certainly not attract or keep college-age young adults. This type of atmosphere widens the back door and shrinks the front door.

A do-it-yourself faith. As we discussed in chapter 1, a disconnect between faith and the church exists. Students are looking for more; they are on a spiritual journey. They are seeking this amorphous thing called faith, but they are not coming to the church to find it. Only 16 percent of dropouts left the church because they desired to leave organized religion. And only 20 percent of teenage students plan to leave the church while in high school. Conversely, 80 percent of these students do not plan to leave. They just fall off the radar after age eighteen. Sadly, at one of the most critical junctions of life, the transition into adulthood, people are separating faith and church. Perhaps one of the most staggering findings in the entirety of our research is how unimportant the church has become with the younger generation.

18 to 22 year olds		
	Dropouts	Those who stay
My church was important to my life[6]	28%	78%

Why do these students take a break from church? It isn't because the college is drawing them away. It's because the church is unimportant to them. We push them away. Why is it so easy for them to leave? The church is not a meaningful part of their lives. Why is the back door so large and the front door so small? The church is nonessential to them. We have left this group of young adults to figure out faith on their own. They are patching together a religious system apart from the church. These dropouts are creating a dangerous, piecemeal personal faith. They find faith in the Internet, in social circles, and through popular books, but for many this faith they find is a farce. They parade it around as if they have become enlightened by some newfound discovery of God. But it is only a charade for age-old lies. The One true God is revealed only through His Word, the Holy Scriptures.

As we will see in the second half of the book, churches must deepen in order to retain college-age students. Between 65 percent and 90 percent of active churchgoers come to church through the witness of a relationship with another person.[7] Relationships are a key component in the health of the church. Membership in a church matters; faith is not disconnected from the church. Faith does not have a do-it-yourself option. People do not make solid spiritual journeys apart from a local body of believers. We do not mosey in a spiritual forest alone. An essential church is one that has a firm foundation based on biblical truth. An essential church is one that conveys clearly the fundamentals of the faith to its students. When this atmosphere disappears, students are left in a fog only to wander from the church that is supposed to convey how they are to walk through this life.

Activity is not the same as being active. If we create a fun activity, they will stay . . . right? Wrong! Many churches fall into the trap of thinking games and other activities will keep students in the church. Indeed, these types of events may help *attract* students from the community who do not know Christ, but they do not help to *assimilate* the students who have been in the church for a period of time. Our study revealed that the vast majority of the survey participants attended many activities in their local church prior to their departure. The chart below demonstrates that many students, including dropouts and those who stay, are active in church functions.

Attendance and participation in church for those under 18	
Regularly attended worship service	86%
Participated in church youth group activities	74%

Attendance and participation in church for those under 18	
Attended small group, Sunday school, or discipleship class	66%
Attended a Christian camp	53%

We were pleased to find that many students were attending worship and involved in church activities. Attendance in these areas, however, did not in themselves prevent their exodus. In other words, these students were engaging in many church *activities*, but they were not necessarily *actively* involved in growing more spiritually mature. So they came, they participated, and then they left.

While most students are participating in church *activities*, relatively few have actual *responsibilities* in their church. The chart below demonstrates the low level of responsibility among those under eighteen.

Responsibility in church for those under 18	
Had regular responsibilities in my church	37%
Held leadership position in the activities of my church	25%

Going to Christian camps, attending youth functions, and being present for worship are important for teens in the church. They should be part of corporate worship and fellowshipping with others their age. If they do not take ownership of their church, however, then they are more inclined to leave when life begins to change drastically for most at age eighteen.

We understand that not every teen can have a leadership role within the church. And many are not ready spiritually to have certain responsibilities. Where the biggest discrepancy is found, however, is in the focus of the church. Is it inward or outward? The church that teaches and disciples all teens to think outwardly has a much better chance of retaining them inwardly.

The chart on the next page breaks down three areas of outward focus within the church. Clearly those churches that have students thinking in terms of service, giving, and missions are more likely to attract and retain the younger generation. Even with those students who stay, we are disappointed that more were not involved in outwardly focused ministries of the church. The spread between the two groups, however, is evident. Healthier churches are more outward churches, and they retain students at a greater rate.

Teenage (younger than 18 years old) involvement in outwardly focused ministries[8]		
	Dropouts	**Those who stay**
Service projects	47%	61%
Consistently giving financially	37%	48%
Mission trips	25%	36%

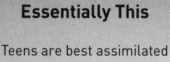

Essentially This

Teens are best assimilated into the church through their service, giving, and missions.

Ministering to young adults is difficult. Assimilating them in the church proves even more complicated. Activity alone is not adequate. Participation, while a step forward, will not help keep college students in the church. This age group must be given responsibilities and leadership positions when they are ready. And most important, the church should be obedient about teaching them one of its essential functions: reaching outward into the community and the world through giving, service, and missions.

Hello. Is there anybody out there? Contrary to the perceptions of parents, educators, and ministers across the globe, teens really do want help with life decisions. They are looking for guidance, even if they never verbalize their desires. And teenagers do look up to adults though they will never admit it.

"You know, my parents seem to know what they're talking about usually, but don't tell them I said that," one teen quipped.

"I think my mom, like, has pretty cool fashion sense. But I'd like *never* ask to borrow her clothes."

"Who knew my dad liked Van Halen!? I didn't even think he knew who they were!"

Teens *are* actually looking for guidance from adults. And yes, somewhere beneath the cynical pubescent veneer is a young adult wanting to hear sound advice. But perhaps more surprising is that they wanted the church to help guide their life decisions. In fact, 57 percent of *all* young adults admitted that prior to turning eighteen they wanted the church to help with everyday decisions in their lives.[9]

The church is missing a grand opportunity to influence the world for Jesus Christ. Many of our students do have some level of desire for the church to help guide their life. The problem is that it can be tough to crack through the shell that many teens hide beneath. But they do want your help. They do want to hear how the church might be able to give them clarity.

Will they listen? Does this guidance affect whether they stay in the church or not? It does. The bottom line: guidance, biblical truth, and responsibility are the missing ingredients. Thirty percent more of those students who stay in the church had a desire to receive guidance from the church. About 20 percent more of those who stay in the church stated they spent regular time reading their Bible privately. And 16 percent more of those teens who stay in the church had responsibilities in their local congregation.[10]

Teens are listening. They're pleading internally for help. Is anybody out there in the church willing to start helping guide them through their life changes?

Don't blame the university. In chapter 1 we debunked the myth of freedom. Students do not leave the church because of a deep desire for personal freedom once out from under their parents' wings. Now we will debunk another myth: it's the university's fault that they're dropping out of church. It's all that secular, humanistic gobbledygook that's forever tainting the fragile Christian minds of our youth! It's the state universities and colleges that are swaying our children away from the biblical principles of our faith! We've all heard such an argument. The problem is that it's simply not true.

There is no significant difference between the dropout rates of those who attend at least a year of college and those who do not. In fact, as the chart below reveals, the dropout rates are almost identical. For those that go to college, 69 percent of active church-

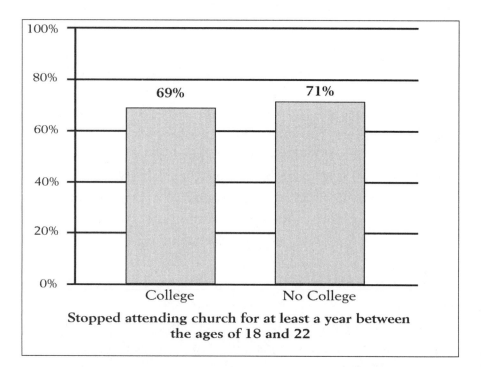

Stopped attending church for at least a year between the ages of 18 and 22

going youth stop attending church for at least a year between the ages of eighteen and twenty-two. Yet 71 percent of active youth who do not go to college stop attending church during the same period. Many do leave at the same time as when they start going to college. But it's a statistical tie; the college itself is not prompting students to drop out of church.

We tend to give secular universities and colleges too much credit in seducing the youngest generation away from the church. Without a doubt, these institutions shape and mold young adults, but they are not a major impetus behind the lack of college students worshipping in churches across the United States. Other research has provided similar results. A study at the University of Texas at Austin found that college students are less likely to abandon their faith than those who never attend college. As we mentioned in chapter 1, faith and church attendance do not necessarily coincide. The point of this research is that religious faith is rarely seen as something that could either influence or be influenced by the educational process.[11]

The University of Texas at Austin researchers stated in their report, "While higher education opens up new worlds for students who apply themselves, it can, but does not often, create skepticism about old (religious) worlds, or at least not among most American young people, in part because students themselves do not perceive a great deal of competition between higher education and faith and also because many young Americans are so undersocialized in their religious faith (before college begins) that they would have difficulty recognizing faith-challenging material when it appears."[12] The myth of the university is broken; colleges are not responsible for church dropouts. The church is responsible for church dropouts.

Our research did reveal that those students attending Christian colleges do have lower dropout rates than average, but it is more driven by the fact that a segment of spiritually stronger teens tend to select Christian schools.

In the end, dropouts who return tend to do so for the same reasons they left: changes that occur in their lives. Some get married and return; others have a child and feel that they need to "get back in church." Sometimes, like with the story of Brian, people have tragic events that prompt them to come back. Church attendance can become a cycle. Life changes; they leave. Life changes; they come back again. Another life change and they may be gone for good.

The essential church breaks this cycle. Churches that become important to the lives of people don't lose many to life changes. Instead, the essential church is part of the healing, part of the process, and part of the fun of all that life can bring. It's time we stopped passing the buck of blame and started looking for ways to solve the problem.

CHAPTER 4

A New Spin on Hypocrisy

What do you mean we can't get on the flight with these tickets?" The anger was building in my (Sam's) voice.

"Sir, the tickets you and your wife have don't appear to be valid," the lady behind the scanner politely replied.

"It's what you guys gave us when we checked in from our departure city; why on earth would they not be valid?"

For whatever reason the plane tickets in our layover city were not scanning correctly. I was scheduled to speak at a conference in a few hours, and I did not want to miss the event. My agitation was apparent to everyone in line behind me. My wife was giving me her look, the "calm down Samuel Solomon Rainer III look." Erin is a gracious woman, a kind woman—but I knew that I would get an earful later.

"OK, what do I have to do to get on *that* plane—the one right out there that I can see from here. Because I'm not moving from this line until we work this out."

"Let me see what I can do, sir." She called a person to help her. About ten minutes later, and just in time to board, the error was corrected. We were on our way.

"You'd better watch your attitude, honey, because you might hinder God's work by being a jerk," my loving wife spoke peremptorily.

Yeah, be a Jesus freak, not a Jesus jerk, something inside me said.

I kept to a guilty quiet until we sat down, my wife with a window seat and me in the middle of the row of three.

"You sure told them," the guy next to me smirked. "These airlines can get at ya."

"Yup." I was still steaming a bit, but I knew I had not accomplished my WWJD mission.

The rest of the flight was uneventful. We three read our books.

"So where you heading?" the guy asked me as we were landing.

"The downtown conference center."

"Oh really, me too."

Then it hit me. Was this guy going to be at the conference where I was to speak?

We were in line together at the same rental car company. Then we saw him checking into our motel. Then we saw him walking to the conference center. Then he went into a different auditorium. The relief came fast, and my sweating subsided.

The irony was that I spoke on the subject matter found in this chapter.

Good thing he didn't ask what I did for a living on the flight. My response of "pastor" might not have been well-received.

Both the unchurched and the churched in America have bemoaned for years the hypocrisy of Christians in the church. And since sinless perfection will not be achieved on this side of eternity, there seems to be little hope to resolve this problem.

But the young dechurched have their own perspective on hypocrisy, and their insights prove valuable in examining this ubiquitous dilemma.

The Parent Trap

The problem of hypocrisy does not begin at the national level. It is not rooted in general perceptions of the church as a whole. It is not perpetuated in amorphous feelings about church people as a collective group. This problem begins a little closer to home. Perhaps one of the most dichotomous results in the research study involved the actions and attitudes that children perceive of their parents. On the one hand, parents have the potential to help keep students in the church. They, as much as any other factor, can help guide and shape their children to become spiritually mature and active in a local body. The problem is that while parents maintain the potential to spark a revival in the hearts of this younger generation, it's not happening. Children are told positive things about the church, but then these same children do not see the church as essential in the lives of their parents. What they hear from parents concerning spirituality and what they see in their lives are two different pictures.

Parents are a critical element in keeping college-age young adults in the church. They are more than mere parental figureheads. These students, even older teens, look closely at how their parents are living out what they say is spiritually important. And how well parents convey the importance of the church plays a major role in whether students remain or drop out. Additionally, parents have the ability to persuade the dechurched to become rechurched. We hope that it is not surprising to find that parents have a profound influence on their children. But our research uncovered a strong link between teens assimilating in the church and the actions of parents. In other words, it isn't enough for your children to *hear* from you that church and spirituality are important. Parents must *show* their children that church is essential to the entire family.

In our surveys most young adults indicated they had positive family perceptions about the church. In other words, their parents were not speaking ill of the body of believers. Most children are raised in homes where the church is viewed in a positive light. In fact, 76 percent of young adults indicate that they had parents or family members who attended church regularly. We admit the term

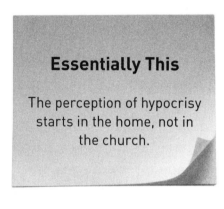

Essentially This

The perception of hypocrisy starts in the home, not in the church.

regularly may mean different things for different people. Pastors typically have a stricter definition of what it means to be regular in a church as compared with many laypeople. Regardless, most children are influenced by others in their families who go to church on occasion. Their opinions about the church are not formed in a vacuum. The younger generation is not totally disconnected from the church, as most have at least one family member who is in some way connected.

Additionally, 73 percent of the younger generation indicated in our research that these parents or family members who attended church were perceived as genuinely liking the church. Such a statistic makes sense: those who go to church clearly should have a genuine liking for that church.

Family influences of all young adults prior to age 18[1]	
Family members or parents attended church regularly	76%
Family members or parents genuinely like the church	73%

The dropout generation picked up on this connection. The family attended church on occasion. Their family liked the church. They had positive feelings about the church. The church was not an institution that was thought of as a bad influence. So the parents and children, with perhaps other family members involved, went to church. It might not be as frequently as church leaders would prefer, but at least they were attending with some level of regularity.

So what happens? If their families are not degrading the church as a worthless institution, then why do 70 percent of those who leave do so between the young ages of eighteen and twenty-two? Why does this exodus happen so close to the time when they are exiting their families' households to form their own?

The dropouts see spiritual hypocrisy in their own family. This perception begins in the home before it carries over to the church in general.

We want to clarify that most children would not call their parents spiritual hypocrites. The term undoubtedly sounds harsh. Nor do we want to berate different parenting styles. We also understand that the family unit does not look like the traditional form in many households, Christian or not. When we use the term *parent*, we also refer to children's guardians.

A definite trend exists in the church. Parents are not doing what they say as it relates to the church body. Or perhaps more appropriately, parents are not saying as they do. While parents are attending church and their children see their actions of being in the worship service, children are not receiving spiritual guidance from their parents.

The new spin on hypocrisy is that "doing church" is not enough. Parents must talk to their children about why church and matters of spirituality are essential. Teens must hear regularly from their parents or guardians as well as seeing their actions. Do as I do, and hear what I say. The spiritual guidance children hear from their parents weighs equally with the actions they see from their parents.

Children see, children do. Anyone who has helped raise children knows well they mimic behavior. And many of you may have funny anecdotes of public jibes that were uttered from your son's or daughter's mouth at some point in their young existence. You may have said it yourself, thinking that your child would never remember to repeat it. Parenting has many high points. Watching your children become young adults is one of life's most rewarding experiences. The mimicking tots soon grow into mocking teenagers.

Both tots and teens, however, mimic behavior. These traits change with the age of your child, but children still follow adult influence throughout their teen years. Church attendance is no exception. Only 19 percent of teens who regularly attend a worship service indicate that their parents or family members do *not* attend church regularly. When teens go to church, most of the time parents are attending as well. Conversely, only 8 percent of teens who had parents or family members attending church regularly indicated that they did *not* attend worship themselves. Therefore, if parents or guardians go to church, most of the time the teens go as well.[2]

Family influence of all young adults prior to age 18	
Teens who attend with parents who do not	19%
Teens who do not attend with parents who do	8%

We were surprised throughout our research at the pervasiveness of this behavioral trend. We cannot overlook the bottom line: the correlation between teen church attendance and parent church attendance is high. Few teens go to church when their parents do not, and fewer teens do not attend church if their parents are going. Clearly, some parents will force a teen to go to church, but the overwhelming factor is that teen church attendance is heavily influenced by the parents' habits. The problem, as expressed previously, is that this mirroring effect degrades after age eighteen. What family dynamics took place to prompt the dropouts to leave? Even within families that regularly attend church, why would young adults leave? Church attendance by the family alone will not help assimilate students. So what specific factors in the family unit other than just church attendance caused the young adult exodus?

The roots of hypocrisy in the family unit. As we stated earlier, prior to age eighteen, many teenagers had connections to the church through family members. And for the most part, these families viewed the church positively. The younger generation perceived their parents and family members as having a genuine liking for their church. In addition, many of these future dropouts attended church with their family. So where's the hypocrisy? The family went to church. They liked the church. What's the problem?

The problem is that teens saw their parents *doing* church but *saying* little about the faith for which their church stands. Whether parents intended to convey it or not, most dropouts perceived church attendance as empty action. Going to church and liking the church are critically important. But those steps are only part of the equation in assimilating students into the local body of believers.

As we discussed in chapter 3, activity in church does not necessarily equate to active churchgoing young adults. Teens are attracted to special events and youth activities. And we would never advocate discarding these types of outward ministries. They are helpful in attracting the unchurched. But mere attendance in church does not cut it. More is needed from the adults in the church, particularly from parents or family members, in order to stem the tide of exiting young adults.

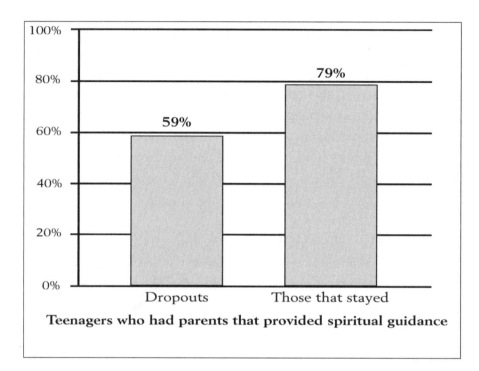

Teenagers who had parents that provided spiritual guidance

The breakdown begins with parents providing spiritual guidance. Pawning off the teaching and discipling of a child to the church without providing parental insight results in a greater chance of that child's dropping out of church. The spread between dropouts and those that stay in the church is large when comparing students who received spiritual guidance from family members and those students who did not. Almost eight out of ten students who stayed in the church stated their parents or family members gave them direct spiritual guidance. In comparison, only 59 percent of those who dropped out indicated they received this guidance from their family members.[3]

While many parents certainly believe they are doing well to get their children and teens in church (and they are!), the children of the church need their parents to talk to them about spiritual matters. The doing of church must be accompanied by the telling of why it's important. This concept is well rooted in the Bible. The going and telling of the gospel message of Jesus

Christ is an imperative. Going to worship with the fellowship of believers is an expectation. But this action should be married with our words. Our church attendance should be coupled with telling others, particularly our children, why our faith in the Messiah has forever changed and impacted our worldview. Our faith is lived. Our faith is told. Our children need to see both sides. Otherwise they are mimicking behavior without truly understanding why involvement in a local church is critical to the spiritual health of a believer.

The roots of perceived Christian hypocrisy dig deep into the family unit. Without direct spiritual guidance, many students never make the connection between church and faith. The church becomes unrelated to the actions and mandates of Jesus because no one within the church exemplified how they tie together. What the church expects and what the students see in their faith become disjointed. The beginning of this "expect one thing and say another" hypocrisy starts with the relationship between parent and child. Actions without words leave this generation wondering why they're attending church.

This disconnect is exemplified in the discrepancy between dropouts and those that stayed. Particularly in the areas of spiritual discussion, service in the church, and prayer, the dichotomy between these two groups is evident. The chart on the following page shows how those church families that engage their students with more than an expectation for church attendance keep young adults at a higher rate.[4]

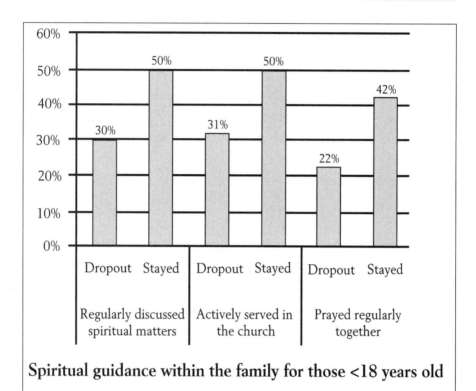

Spiritual guidance within the family for those <18 years old

Half of those students that stayed in church stated in our survey that their family discussed spiritual matters, as compared with only 30 percent of those that dropped out of church. Additionally, half of those students who were assimilated into the church indicated that their family actively served in the church, as compared with only 31 percent of dropouts. And lastly, 42 percent of those whom the church retained stated that their family prayed together regularly, as compared with only 22 percent of those who dropped out. The openness of spiritual discussion within the family helps dissolve any feelings of frustrations from the younger generation. When parents are open about their spiritual struggles and successes, teens are less likely to see hypocrisy.

Indirect hypocrisy creeps into the church when many attend but never commit to serving the church body. The concept of taking and receiving from the church is perpetuated when parents do not demonstrate this service to their children. The false idea of church being a place where people receive instead of give continues. The youth of the church should see a sacrificial spirit lived out in the lives of the adults in the church. When what they see in their family matches what is preached every Sunday, the potential for hypocritical perceptions is quelled.

Prayer is the cornerstone of every ministry in the church. The church's support is found in the prayers of its people. Ministerial success is rooted in tapping into God's power. This spirit of prayer also works in the lives of the younger generation. When families pray together, the Holy Spirit works. While it is impossible to quantify the working of the Holy Spirit, there is an undeniable correlation between prayer and assimilation. Families that begin to pray together will find only spiritual successes in the lives of their children as a result of those prayers.

While our discussion has centered on families that attend church, our research also revealed insights about those parents who do not attend church but have children who do attend. Nearly a third of those students who dropped out of church stated that their family expressed good intentions about church but rarely attended. These students faced the brunt of hypocrisy surrounding church—families that say it's a good thing to go but never did so themselves. Parents who drop off children at church should not be surprised when their children drop out and cite the hypocrisy of everyone in the church. In these cases where a student is involved in a local church without his or her family, the church should invest several adults in helping disciple him or her.

The harmony effect. The fabric of the family unit is frayed. Divorce rates are high. Many children grow up in single-parent homes. But the purpose of this section is not to point fingers. Every situation is unique. Each family has its own story. While we do not intend to pass judgment, we do want to relay the facts about family harmony and how it affects the dropout rates of the younger generation. The greater degree of harmony found within the family unit, the higher the chance of students staying in the church.

Description of parents at age 17[5]		
	Dropouts	Those who stay
My parents were still married	52%	70%
My parents had the same religious preference	49%	64%
My parents had the same denominational preference	40%	55%
My parents attended the same church	36%	58%

Those that remained active in church as young adults reported at higher rates their parents were still married to each other. While 70 percent of those that stayed in church indicated their parents were still married, only 52 percent of those that dropped out stated their parents were still married to each other. If parents stay together until their child turns seventeen, then the greater the likelihood he or she will remain in the church.

Not only will parents staying together affect the stability of their teens' church activity, but religious preference also plays a major role. Dropouts indicated at much lower rates that their parents had the same religious preferences. When parents are unified about religion, their children have a much greater chance of assimilation in the local church. While less of a factor, denominational harmony with the parents also plays a role in keeping children in church. More of those students who stayed in church indicated that their parents gravitated toward the same denomination.

Attending the same church is perhaps the best way for parents to relay to their children their harmony on religious matters. Almost six out of ten students who stayed in their church said their parents attended the same church. In comparison, only 36 percent of those who dropped out stated their parents went to the same church. We conclude that the greater the religious harmony with the parents, the less chance their children will become confused as to which church they should attend or if they should drop out.

One of the best ways for families to combat the perceptions of hypocrisy is to become proactive in teaching children spiritual disciplines, being consistent in lifestyle, and remaining authentic in their struggles. The combination of these three factors does play a factor in keeping the younger generation in church. On average, 20 percent more of those who stay indicate that their families practiced this spiritual proactivity and transparency. In order for these practices to have the full effect, parents must be both genuine in their efforts and regular in practice. The church can become essential to the younger generation once again. But the process begins in the home. Once this generation sees that there is no hypocrisy in the home, then hypocrisy in the church is more easily combated.

The Problem in the Pews

While the pervasive problem of hypocrisy in the church begins in the home, it swells to new levels in the church. We've all heard about how the world claims the church is full of hypocrites. Sometimes these comments are cop-outs; other times they are fully warranted. Much of the world believes that in order to belong to a church, one must be to some extent a hypocrite. Outsiders have long claimed that those on the inside of the church

do not live out what they say they believe. In the younger generation 84 percent of those who are not in church claim that they
know a committed Christian. We rejoice that so many people have
contact with others who know Jesus Christ. The latent potential
for revival waits. The problem is that while 84 percent of these
outsiders know a Christian, only 15 percent of them see a marked
change in their lifestyle from the rest of the secular world![6]

We all wear masks. At some point most of us can admit
that we have shed our own standards to compromise on a selfish desire. The term *hypocrite* actually refers to the wearing of a
mask; the term is derived from a Greek word. In ancient Greek
culture, the actors of the day were "hypocrites." They wore masks
when they played different acting roles. These masks enabled
them to shield their true identity in order to take on differing
personas for the sake of entertaining the masses.

We like to wear masks so we can tickle the ears of others with
little repercussions. We tell people what they want to hear whether
we believe it or not. At some point we've all played a part on life's
stage that we knew we should not have played. Transparency does
not come naturally. It takes work to be honest with who you are.

Such is the dilemma of a Christian. We are called to be set
apart. Yet we are also called to be in the world. The extremes of
legalism and relativism entice us. Many Christians set up such
strict religious parameters that the world, looking at their lives,
sees a prison. The legalistic fences they erect make the Bible seem
to be full of razor wire. Stay away or get spiritually sliced to bits.
Christ warned the Pharisees about locking up the kingdom of
heaven (see Matt. 23:13). Our Lord had harsh words to say about
empty ritual and rank legalism.

The outside world looks at legalism as hypocrisy. They know
that we are supposed to reach out. Yet we build walls instead. We
remain inward, driven by our selfish desires to focus on personal
spiritual boot camp.

Even more problematic and widespread is the tendency toward spiritual laxity. Obvious sins that were once regarded as clearly taboo are creeping up the ladder of acceptability within the younger generation. Six out of ten born-again believers ages twenty-three to forty-one now state that cohabitation is morally acceptable. Four out of ten believe sex outside of marriage is morally acceptable. Three out of ten believe pornography is morally acceptable.[7] With the extremes of legalism and moral laxity so prevalent within the circles of Christianity, it is no wonder that outsiders look at the church as a hypocritical bunch.

The claim that outsiders will never truly grasp Christianity because they are not Christians themselves carries some validity. But the claim of "the world just doesn't get it" painfully belly flops when looking at the stinging indictment of what occurs on the inside of our churches.

The Damaging Effects of Hypocrisy

It's not the outsiders we should be most concerned about at this point. Undoubtedly their perceptions are crucial when reaching a lost world for Christ. But more important at this juncture are those who are currently on the inside. We first presented the chart on the next page in chapter 1. We stated that an essential church is an authentic church. A church that keeps its students is one that is transparent with them about the realities of Christianity. This chart clearly demonstrates the difference between the churches of those that stay and those that do not from the perception of our own students.

Percent of 18 to 22 year olds who maintain these impressions about their church[8]		
	Those who stayed	**Those who dropped out**
Caring	74%	39%
Welcoming	71%	36%
Authentic	67%	30%
Inspirational	56%	20%
Insincere	19%	41%
Judgmental	24%	51%

A caring, welcoming, authentic, and inspirational church is much more likely to assimilate its students. Conversely, the churches that do not demonstrate these biblical qualities, but rather become inflexible and judgmental, lose this generation. They return to the culture that claims churches are not living up to their calling. And, for the most part, the culture is correct. We're losing students on the inside because our churches are not fulfilling their purpose to the outside world. These students leave because they *hear* one thing preached and then they *see* another thing lived out in the lives of the people. They hear about the fruit of the Spirit, yet this same level of caring and kindness is not exemplified within the church. Yes, we need to be greatly concerned about outside perceptions. But perhaps more frightening are what our own students are saying about our churches. Reaching outsiders is critical to the survival of the church, but we have a generational crisis with church health on the inside. And what better way to get healthy on the inside than to start showing our own students that we care deeply about those on the outside. Start reaching out into the community and begin to heal inwardly.

The effects of this hypocrisy produce damaging results on the spiritual welfare of our younger generation. Admittedly, not all dropouts leave because of heightened levels of hypocrisy in the church. And not every student struggles with discipleship because the adults in the church do not follow through with their own spiritual maturation. But many of the same students who attend an uncaring, insincere, and judgmental church also practice spiritual disciplines much less. God's Word speaks for itself. The dropouts will be held accountable for their actions, but the church will also be held accountable for not providing a climate and atmosphere in which students can grow spiritually.

Our research revealed a sobering outcome: dropouts never developed strong spiritual habits. They practice spiritual disciplines much less than their peers who stay in church. Not only is the church losing a younger generation, but we are also watching a spiritually immature generation amalgamate with the world. The back doors of our churches are wide—an entire generation flowing through churches without ever grasping the magnitude of their decision to leave. They see a church full of people who differ little from the world. And they go into a hostile culture armed minimally with God's armor. The chart below reveals the distinction between those who leave and the students who are assimilated into the church. From this information we gather a weighty conclusion: spiritual discipline is sorely lacking in nonessential churches.

Personal desires and activities related to church between the ages of 18 and 22[9]		
	Those who stayed	Dropouts
Strong belief system in place	83%	56%
Regular time spent in prayer	80%	44%
Bible guides everyday decisions	78%	30%
Regular time spent in reading the Bible	63%	29%

Of those teens who had a strong belief system in place, 27 percent more stayed in their churches. Of the teens who spend regular time in prayer, 36 percent more stayed in their churches. Only 30 percent of those students who dropped out desired for the Bible to guide everyday decisions. Almost the same percentage of dropouts indicated that they spent regular time reading the Bible.

Hypocrisy hurts more than just the perception of the church from the outside. Our own students and children pick up on the double-talk. Teens are savvy. They may be less mature than a bill-paying adult, but their internal radar picks up hypocrisy with pinpoint accuracy. Many of our churches are self-defeating. The influences of secular society do exacerbate the problem, but the real answer does not rest with defeating these cultural pressures. The church's battle is not against the culture. We fight not against men but against the powers of darkness.

> For our battle is not against flesh and blood, but against
> the rulers, against the authorities, against the world
> powers of this darkness, against the spiritual forces of evil
> in the heavens. (Eph. 6:12)

Our churches should be about the business of reaching the fallen world. We do stand firm against sin, but more important we stand for Jesus Christ and the Word of God. It's time our students began to see what our churches stand for, as well as what we stand against, for this generation will never understand what we fight against unless we show them how we live for Christ.

The problem of hypocrisy begins close to home. Indeed, it begins in the home. The problem in the pews exacerbates the hypocrisy seen in the home. The news about hypocrisy is that "doing church" is not enough. We all need to live up to our callings as the church. Essential churches show by example that they are what they claim. Their vision statements become their reality statements. Students that drop out of essential churches have a clear grasp of what they are leaving. Unfortunately most students leave nonessential churches, and they have no idea about the gravity of the decision to leave the fellowship of believers.

It's time to stop blaming the world and take a deep look on the inside of our churches. The world has an influence, but the greater effects that occur on the lives of our younger generation occur within the church. The blame cannot be shifted on a decadent culture. Since the blame lies in our court, however, we can stop the spinning of hypocrisy. We have the potential to change course. The mass exodus of students can be stopped. Through the guidance of the Holy Spirit, we can reverse the general perceptions of hypocrisy emanating from our own students. And our churches can put the old spin of the unchanging gospel message back on the world. Once equipped, our students can then lead the charge against the powers of darkness and engage a world for Jesus Christ.

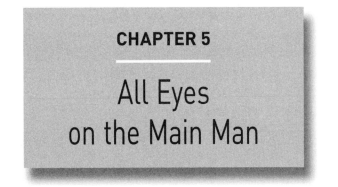

CHAPTER 5

All Eyes
on the Main Man

A recent Sunday started with me (Sam) lying on the bath-room floor at five. The severe pains in my lower back and stomach prevented me from standing. I knew that it might not be one of my better Sundays. But as you probably can imagine, finding a replacement for the pulpit is not an easy task early Sunday morning.

I wasn't feeling sick. No nausea. I didn't have to do the tur-key trot. But the pain was severe. I managed to lumber off the floor and get ready for church.

I think I can make it through the day.

Bad decision number one.

Once I arrived and settled in my office, the pins and needles subsided. I went about my normal routine. Halfway through my Sunday school class, I stopped teaching and grimaced in pain once again. Of course, the class wanted to know what was wrong.

I told them of my symptoms: waves of pain in my lower back and stomach, but no typical stomach bug symptoms.

Reggie, an Indiana state trooper, interjected, "Do you drink a lot of diet sodas?"

"I live off them," I replied.

"You probably don't drink a lot of water, either, do you?"

"Nope."

What is this, some sort of health survey?

"Do you eat peanuts?"

"Yes, I snack on them quite a bit."

Peanuts?! Where is he going with this?

"You've got kidney stones!" Reggie exclaimed in quasi-joy at his perceived correct diagnosis.

Kidney stones? No way, I'm too young to have kidney stones.

I did match the symptoms. And all of a sudden my day got worse.

My associate pastor peeked into my office before the service to see how I was doing.

"You gonna make it, my man?"

"I think so."

"I've got an old sermon ready if you need me to step in," he graciously offered.

"Nah, I got it covered."

The pricking pains continued, but I figured as long as I could manage the pain I could putter my way through a sermon.

Bad decision number two.

I entered the service at about 75 percent to a larger-than-usual crowd. My lower back loosened the grip of knots, and I worshipped without much problem.

Then our music minister led the congregation in "Amazing Grace."

Sweat began to pour off my nose. My hands and arms went numb. My legs tingled. And the pain returned with a fury.

I sat down.

A deacon came up to me and asked if I was OK.

I waived him away.

Bad decision number three.

The song ended, and I waddled into the pulpit. I warned the congregation that I wasn't feeling well, and I asked them to bear with me.

It was the only good decision of the day.

For some reason God gave me the strength to preach through half my sermon without much happening. At the halfway point, God gave me divine insight. It came as a rumbling in my tummy.

Uh-oh. I don't have kidney stones. I really do *have the stomach flu.*

I swayed and slurred my way to point number four. Point number four was the quickest point I've ever made in a sermon.

Nature's call was going to take precedence over the sermon today.

I abruptly ended and called for someone to close the service.

At this point in the story I blacked out. The details you see in the following section were filled in by my loving and understanding church.

Apparently I made it backstage where I promptly passed out and puked everywhere. It was a righteous spew.

I came to in a halfway state of semiconsciousness with the chairman of the deacons holding me up and one of the personnel committee members scrubbing the floor around me. I vaguely remember thinking something about washing people's feet, but somehow I think both of them would rather have washed my feet.

"You all right?" the deacon asked.

"Yeah, I think I'll be fine. Did the service end OK?" I asked faintly.

"Well, we all knew you were sick."

"Really, you could tell?"

"Well, we all heard ya . . ."

"Was I that loud?"

Here I learned of bad decision number four. It was this slip that has been the buzz of the church.

My deacon hesitantly answered my question, "Mmm, I think you forgot to turn your mic off."

You are probably laughing at my expense. But I tell this story to make a point: leaders are visible people. My bad decisions had an effect on many more people than just myself. The whole church felt my case of the stomach flu.

Perhaps my associate pastor summed up the whole episode best: "Sam, that was the most unholy thing that I've ever heard come out of your mouth."

The leaders of the church are one of the most visual aspects of the local body. And the pastor of the church is the most visible of all leaders in the local body. And the time in which he is most visible is during the sermon. While lay leaders and other staff persons hold critical roles in the church, it is the lead pastor to whom most people look. He is the main man. All eyes are on him.

This scrutiny is not limited to the adults of the church. Our research indicates that the eighteen- to twenty-two-year-old age group is measuring up the pastor as well, if not more so. Those who have dropped out of church relayed to us through our research and interviews that they looked carefully at the man they called "pastor" in their church while growing up. Whether their pastor was cognizant that they even existed, he had an impact on their lives during their formative years.

What was disheartening about our research is that the pastor left this young age group desiring more from him than they received. He made an impact, but for many of those who dropped out, it was a negative impact. The young eyes of the church examined him, and they did not like what they saw.

The Buck Stops in the Pulpit

While almost all dropouts indicated a life change was a major reason for their departure, 58 percent of dropouts also stated they left their local body because of church-related or pastor-related issues. The chart below reveals three broad categories of specific reasons dropouts exit their church.

Categories of specific reasons church dropouts (18 to 22) leave[1]	
Life changes	97%
Church- or pastor-related reasons	58%
Religious, ethical, or political beliefs	52%

Well over half of the dropouts were looking to the leaders of the church, and they came away wanting. As we saw in chapter 3, this generation of church dropouts is looking for guidance from the church. They want the leaders to help shape and mold their lives in a positive fashion. Even though they do not vocalize it, and at times they will balk at help, this generation has a deep desire to be influenced by more spiritually mature adults within the church.

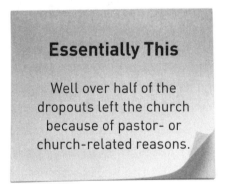

Essentially This

Well over half of the dropouts left the church because of pastor- or church-related reasons.

The leadership of the church, particularly the lead or senior pastor, is the linchpin for this catalyst of cross-generational discipleship to occur. Without the guidance and care from the main vision-casting person in the church, dropouts recognize that they have been relegated to a second or third tier of importance. The teenage population is one that knows well the principle of unity in diversity—a principle that should be exercised heavily in our churches.

> From Him the whole body, fitted and knit together by
> every supporting ligament, promotes the growth of the
> body for building up itself in love by the proper working of
> each individual part. (Eph. 4:16)

Each individual part of a church contributes to the fulfilling of the Great Commission and the Great Commandment. Each person plays a pivotal part in seeing the imperative to go into the world fulfilled. Churches should be the one place where a person feels as if he or she is contributing to something greater, that their small role is magnified by God for His mission. When the pastor lowers the bar of expectations for the youth of the church, he is not only missing out on an opportunity for better assimilation, but he is also telling this age group that their contributions are of secondary importance.

The buck stops with the pastor. He holds the primary shepherding responsibility in the church. It is incumbent upon him to empower the youth or to give such responsibility to other leaders who help assimilate this group into the church. The leadership within the church must create an atmosphere in which all people are encouraged and expected to be a vital part of the fellowship.

The church inevitably takes on the characteristics and personality of its leaders. And when the students of the church begin to see that they are not essential to the health because of the focus of the leaders, they pack up and head out of a church that is nonessential to them. As with many group dynamics, if the leaders of the church view a segment of the body as less important, the church typically follows with that same view. If the pastor spends little or no time focusing on the youth of the church, then the church has no reason to believe that it is a worthwhile endeavor to engage that age group.

Prove it to me. Mark wrote his Gospel with a Roman audience in mind. The Romans were not that interested in the prophecies of the Old Testament. They knew little about Hebrew history. What they did want to know was what Jesus did. They were people of action, interested in the works of the Suffering Servant. Sure, what Jesus said was significant, but their curiosity peaked when Mark discussed the miracles and actions of the God-Man. Therefore, Mark penned Peter's eye-witness accounts in speedy bullet-point fashion. He hit the high points. He gave the executive summary of all of Jesus' works. No eloquence. Just the facts, ma'am. Thus, the shortest of the four Gospels has only sixteen chapters, much more condensed when compared to the other two synoptics and John.

Why would Mark write his Gospel account in this way? He knew his audience, and it was the best way to reach them. He understood the Roman culture of "prove it to me by what you do, not by what you say." The Romans needed to hear about Jesus' works, so Mark focused on the means of writing that would best communicate the gospel to them.

"I come from a country that raises corn and cotton, cockleburs and Democrats, and frothy eloquence neither convinces nor satisfies me. I'm from Missouri, and you have got to show me."[2] The phrase, spoken by Congressman Willard Duncan Vandiver in an 1899 speech, popularized the Midwestern state's motto, "The Show-Me State." The phrase stuck and is now arguably the most well-known of all the state mottos. Historically Missourians were natural skeptics. Teenagers might as well all be from Missouri. Like the Romans of ancient time, the latest generation is the "show-me" generation.

Teens are naturally skeptical. They are an overmarketed, oversold, underestimated, and misunderstood generation. They know when you're trying to sell something to them. They have noses that can smell insincerity a mile away. They are attracted to genuineness even if they don't agree with whatever it is.

For them the journey is more fun than the destination. They're tired of the same old baby-boomer drabble. They aren't attracted to cookie-cutter formulas, and they value things that are different. "Frothy eloquence" doesn't satisfy them. And that's just how they feel about the pastor of their church.

This generation wants us to prove to them why the church is essential to their lives. If we build it, they won't necessarily come. If we plan an activity, there's no guarantee that they will assimilate into the church. Teens are looking to the leaders of the church to show them how the church is important to their daily existence. They want to see the importance, relevance, and atmosphere played out in the lives of others in the church. These teens look for the proof in the pudding. They have to taste it and see it before they believe that the church is an essential ingredient to their lives. The chart below reveals the difference between essential churches that reach out to this age group and nonessential churches that relegate teens to a lower rung on the priority ladder.

Statements about church with which 18 to 22 year olds agree[3]		
	Dropouts	Those who stay
My church is important to my life.	54%	76%
The pastor's sermons are relevant to my life.	42%	63%
The worship style of the church is appealing to me.	49%	69%
My church is welcoming to me.	54%	73%

Essential churches show the younger generation why participating in a local church body is critical to the spiritual walk of an individual. As demonstrated in the earlier chart, essential churches keep students in the local body:

- 22 percent more of those who stay indicate they agree that their church is important in their life (54 percent vs. 76 percent).
- 21 percent more of those who stay in church indicate they agree that the pastor's sermons are relevant to their life (42 percent vs. 63 percent).
- 20 percent more of those who continue attending indicate they agree that the worship style is appealing to them (49 percent vs. 69 percent).
- 19 percent more of those who stay indicate they agree that their church is a welcoming environment (54 percent vs. 73 percent).

Pastors of essential churches equip their local fellowship to engage the young adults where they are. They slowly infuse the DNA of importance, relevance, appeal, and welcoming ambiance. These pastors create an informal culture within the church that reaches out to the next generation without being phony or appearing to try too hard. This culture trickles down into the congregation. Good leaders get it done via osmosis. The church wakes up one Sunday morning only to realize they are now relevant to the lives of people in the congregation and in the community.

Creating such a culture is not easy, but it is necessary to stem the tide of college students flowing out of our churches. Like Mark writing his Gospel with a Roman audience in mind, so, too, should pastors and leaders within the church think about where they should meet teens in order best to communicate the saving message of Jesus. The point of the Acts 1:8 imperative is to communicate to a changing world the unchanging message of Jesus Christ. If pastors do not lead churches to contextualize this unchanging message to students, they may find that the people in their pews simply keep getting older and grayer.

Living for the moment, spiritually bankrupt in the future. Ashley Revell, a thirty-two-year-old man from London, knows what it means to live for the moment at the great risk of sacrificing the future.[4] In April 2004 he approached a roulette wheel in Las Vegas with one chip in his hand. The chip represented everything he owned. Donning a rented tuxedo, he placed the chip on red.

Previously that year Ashley had sold everything he possessed (including his underwear, according to the report). On a whim, he decided to "double or nothing" his entire life. The event was recorded by British television for a one-time reality show. The spinning ball in the roulette wheel would double his $135,300 if it fell on red. If the ball skipped into a black slot, Ashley would walk away with literally nothing. Even the rented tux would have to be returned.

Luckily (in the truest sense of the word), the ball slotted red. Everyone cheered. People back in London watching the television celebrated. The press put a positive spin on the story, making Ashley a fifteen-minute hero that week.

"So it was just a mad thing to do," he said.

Ashley walked away from the table twice as rich. He didn't place another bet.

The heartache and burden that this man could have placed upon his family went largely ignored because he won. Our culture tends to do this. We ignore potential problems if we're winning in the here and now. We don't like to think about the risks involved if things are going our way. But such a train of thought is foolish thinking for the church.

> God, You know my foolishness, and my guilty acts are
> not hidden from You. (Ps. 69:5)

We cannot neglect investing in future generations just because of successes now. Healthier, growing churches will only decline at some point in the future without reaching the student generation. Unhealthy, dying churches can slow, stop, and reverse their decline by attracting and keeping the younger generation. It is only foolishness for church leaders and pastors to keep gambling on baby-boomer transfer growth when an entire generation is leaving the church or, worse yet, never knowing the church.

To clarify, we are not advocating a neglect of more mature generations, whether it is the greatest generation, the baby boomers, or Gen Xers. Older and grayer is not bad if those with a little more life experience in the church are using it to benefit those with a little less sagacity. Much can be gained if pastors use and train adults in the church to reach out to those in younger generations.

One of the great blunders of leaders is not investing in the future. The temptation is to live in the moment and not see what steps need to occur in order to lead the church into the future. The risks are too great for us to gamble on not reaching another generation for Christ. The stakes are too high if the youngest generation keeps walking away from the local body of believers. Ignoring this exodus is foolish. It's just a mad thing to do.

Part of the problem for pastors is one of connection. Many leaders in the church think that they do not have time to invest in another segment of the church. In fact, the pastor can be viewed as out of touch with the students of the church not because he is incapable of relating to them. Rather, he's out of touch because he doesn't invest time and effort into them. We believe most pastors have the capacity to reach this generation, but too often the added effort to do so is pawned off onto others in the church.

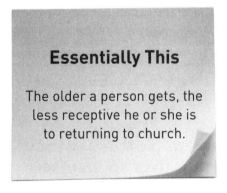

Essentially This

The older a person gets, the less receptive he or she is to returning to church.

Like individuals who carefully plan for retirement, saving portions of their income in order to live with relative ease in their latter years, so too should church leaders invest carefully in the next generation within the local body. This process eases the burden for future leaders in reaching the following generation. Conversely, when leaders in the church neglect to disciple the younger generation, this generation is more apt to leave the church before they become adults. And they become harder to reach later in life. Our research shows that nearly six out of ten people over the age of sixty-five will not consider returning to church. Yet the receptivity rate of younger adults is much higher. In fact, 60 percent of formerly churched eighteen- to thirty-five-year-olds are willing to return to church if a friend or acquaintance invited them. Now is the time to start reaching young adults and college students who have dropped out of church. The longer pastors wait, the longer they gamble on current growth, the more risks they are taking in not reaching the next generation.

Understandably the senior pastor cannot personally invest in every student in the church, especially in larger churches. But a culture of caring for, training up, and relating to this younger generation starts at the top and filters down through the body of the church. If the pastor does not champion this type of investment in the church, then the church is not as likely to view it as essential.

How important is it for pastors to start this investing process? As seen in the following graph, those churches that have leaders investing time in students are more likely to keep them through college and into adulthood. Twenty percent more of those that stayed in the church indicated that they had an adult regularly helping them to grow more spiritually mature. Conversely, 20 percent less of dropouts stated they had this same type of involvement. This adult-teen interaction typically does not occur

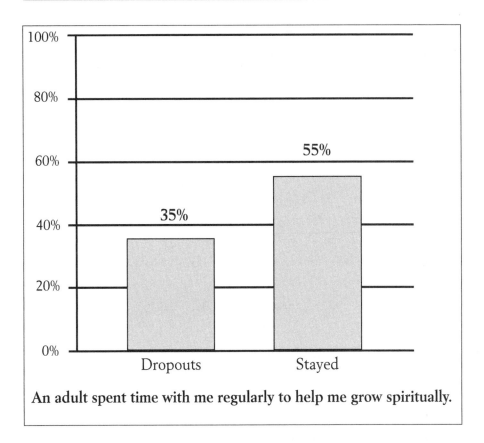

An adult spent time with me regularly to help me grow spiritually.

organically. It is not something that adults in the church gravitate toward naturally. Some adults do feel called to work with these students, but many more do not. The pastor and leaders of the church must make visible efforts to begin connecting adults with teens in small-group settings to encourage this dynamic to take place.

Perhaps this research finding is not surprising to you. Indeed, it almost seems common sense that the more spiritually mature adults help disciple the younger generation, the more likely the younger generation is going to view their church as essential. What might surprise you, as it did us, is how strong the correlation is between this relationship of students and adults.

Number of adults making a significant investment in a teen's life between the ages of 15 and 18[5]	
	% Dropping Out
Zero	89%
One	76%
Two	68%
Three or Four	59%
Five or Six	57%
Seven or More	50%

As the chart above so clearly indicates, the more adult leaders who are investing in a teen's life, the more likely that teen is to stay in church. The more adults who are involved in a teen's life, the lower the dropout rate. In fact, our research reveals that if a teen has no adult interaction in the church, it's almost a guarantee he or she will drop out of the church. Evidenced in the research, those teens with zero adult involvement have a nine-out-of-ten probability of dropping out of the church. Additionally, those teens with multiple adults helping them grow have only a fifty-fifty probability of dropping out.

Pastors be warned: simply relegating the youth ministry to the youth minister is not enough. You must be personally involved in this ministry in order best to assimilate these students into your church. While pastors cannot be expected to disciple every student personally, without the main leader in the church championing the cause of students, most adults will continue to let these students fall to the student ministry without much involvement from others in the church.

But the great news about this research is the simplicity of keeping students. A pastor can reduce the dropout rate of teens from an almost certainty of losing students to only a 50-percent

chance simply by getting adults involved in their lives! No complicated process. No cookie-cutter formula. No huge program. No
expensive resources. Just start encouraging adults and teens to
mix with one another through existing church events. That's it.
All eyes are on the main man. Now's the time to start letting the
people of the church know that putting their eyes on the students
of the church will make their church a healthier body of believers. Invest in the future. Save some time for the students of the
church. Get others excited about what the future will bring, and
change the lives of spiritually bankrupt teens forever.

Servant leadership. Adult involvement encouraged and cham-
pioned from the leaders of the church is a necessity. And this
interaction can greatly improve the spiritual health of teens in
your church. But it isn't the only part of the equation. As we
stated, even with adult interaction the dropout rate remains high
at about 50 percent. Something else is needed to reduce further
the number of those that leave the church as they enter college.

Caring, authentic, real, welcoming, and *inspirational* were
among those characteristics with the highest factors of helping
keep students in the church. These students also desire to see
the pastor and other leaders exemplify these Christlike qualities
as servant leaders in the church.

In his book *Understanding Church Growth*, Donald McGavran
discusses a somewhat controversial subject: the homogeneous
unit. This unit is simply a section of society in which all the
members have some characteristic in common.[6] The basic principle is that people congregate with others like themselves. And
people naturally build barriers around these groups. By default,
groups of people will erect invisible societal walls. These walls
can be harmless, as with a cluster of college students hanging out
with people their age. Or these walls can be horrible blights upon
society, such as the Indian caste system. Students, by default and
design, are part of a homogeneous unit. They build walls like the
rest of us.

One of the best ways to reach the teen culture is to meet them where they are instead of pulling their culture toward where you are. Breaking through these walls is best accomplished by being a servant leader.

In some small way, I (Sam) saw last year how homogeneous units can play out for good. The one calendar event for our church that confused me was upon us: the teenage girls' Get Real Fashion Show. I don't have a problem with fashion shows, but I didn't understand the purpose of the event. The event goes something like this: teens from our church invite other teens from the neighboring high schools to show off the latest styles and how to dress modestly in them.

Several leaders in the church volunteered to help put on the event. And the guys in our church served the girls by doing sound, stage, and lighting. But something happened that night. We had dozens of female guests who otherwise would not have come to our church. They came because it was a nonintrusive way to get to know others in the church who were like them. They came because they knew they would be with others with similar interests and backgrounds. They came because the event was geared specifically for their teenage subculture. They came because several servant leaders in the church made the event happen.

So not only did I see how homogenous units can be used for God's glory, but I also saw how servant leadership aids the process of breaking down walls. You won't lead people unless they trust your leadership. And you build their trust by genuinely serving them. This service reveals your heart. They see that you are willing to be vulnerable and open on their behalf.

What's a good way to reach your teenage community? Understand the walls your church has built. Realize that others build walls too; some are bad, others are harmless. And then look to serve these students where they are. Be open and honest with them. You've got to get behind these walls before people will listen to you. You will never lead them unless they buy in to your leadership.

By the way, religious wrecking balls only make this younger generation incensed that you've tried to destroy their wall. So serve this age group, pray for them, learn where they're coming from, offer opportunities specifically for them, and then watch your church grow the way God wants it to grow.

Is preaching still important? Yes! Even in today's hyper-techno-driven conversational-wiki-culture, preaching is of the utmost importance. Of the several church-related or pastor-related issues noted by dropouts, preaching came up several times as a critical issue in retaining college students and young adults.

As mentioned in chapter 1, one of the most critical ways in which the pastor connects with the students of the church is directly through the sermon. While most think that students are turning off the sermon, tuning into something different, and dropping out of the church, nothing is farther from the truth. Students in the church, both high school and college, view the pastor's sermon with a level of importance. They have their eyes on him and what he is saying to them (or not saying to them, for that matter).

Biblical truth must be conveyed to all age groups, especially through the sermon. Shockingly, students desire for the pastor to preach to them! The problem is not their willingness to listen. Rather, the problem is the fact that the pastor is not engaging them where they are. The following charts reveal how two separate age groups view the importance of their pastor's sermons.

What those under 18 say about their pastor's sermons[7]		
	Dropouts	Those who stay
My pastor's sermons are engaging.	48%	65%
My pastor's sermons are relevant to my life.	42%	63%

Not only are the pastor's sermons critical to the assimilation of those under eighteen (previous chart), but they also gain a level of importance with those between the ages of eighteen and twenty-two (following chart). In other words, the older teens become, the more important it is for the pastor to relate to them through the weekly sermons. As seen in these two charts, the spread between dropouts and those who stay increases with the age of the student. This spread is driven by how well the pastor's sermons relate and engage each of these specific age groups.

What those 18 to 22 say about their pastor's sermons[8]		
	Dropouts	Those who stay
My pastor's sermons are engaging.	35%	72%
My pastor's sermons are relevant to my life.	34%	73%

Particularly with those over eighteen, how well a pastor engages and relates to this age group correlates directly with how long they will stay in the church. Don't make the mistake of thinking that these teens will "grow into" the message you preach. Our research proves the opposite: the older the teen, the more critical it is to reach them at their stage in life. Rather than creating sermons for the forty-five and above crowd, gear sermons or segments of sermons specifically for the teens in your church. The pastor's sermon, largely forgotten in this conversational dialogue about the future of the church, still remains one of the linchpins in keeping students in the church. As a result, the buck still stops in the pulpit with this generation.

The Myth of the Media

The pastor has the potential to be a catalyst for church health. He also holds the potential to lead the church away from spiritual health. Most who hold leadership positions in any capacity at a church know well that people in the body can get upset with the direction of the church, whether good or bad.

And warranted or not, one major factor for disillusionment with the church is the view of the pastor. As stated in the previous section, the buck stops with the senior pastor. He's perceived as the main man leading the Lord's flock. While this potential disillusionment with the lead pastor may not come as a huge surprise, the driving force behind this perception was a shock.

We've all seen the media attention given to scandals within megachurches centering upon failures of the senior pastor. And there is no need to dredge up the specifics of these failures within the scope of this book. Most reading this book will be fairly aware of the details of these instances.

A myth exists about this media attention. Throughout the book we make a point of debunking several myths concerning students and the church. Now we want to expose yet another myth: students are not leaving the church because of the attention given to these scandals. While a media melee usually accompanies these large-scale evangelical failures of church leadership, students do not leave the church because of them. In fact, only 15 percent of those who feel displeasure with the church say it's because of a moral or ethical failure of the leaders.[9]

While some of this media attention may affect those on the outside of the church, it has a minimal effect on those students already in the church. It's not the small amount of national scandals receiving large doses of media attention that push students away from the church. The real reason these students are disenchanted with the position of the pastor hits a little closer to home. The factors contributing most to less-than-favorable views of the pastor were insincerity, judgmental behavior, and a lack of good preaching.[10] In other words, blame cannot be passed on to the media. Rather, the blame lies with the person closest to this generation: the pastor himself. If students maintain an unfavorable view of the pastor, then most likely this perception is driven by the pastor's own actions, his own lack of preaching directly to them (or poor preaching in general), and his own insincerity toward this age group.

The excellence factor. The younger generation has evolved to use a cornucopia of tools in one of the greatest informational revolutions of all time. With access to media—Web sites, sermon podcasts, GodTube videos, and now downloadable books with Amazon's *Kindle*—we have an endless stream of information available to us on an infinite number of subjects. Card catalogues . . . remember those clunky things in the corner of the library? No more. The experts used to know *where* to find data. Now we're all experts at finding data. Information on every subject matter imaginable has become ubiquitous. The new experts discern *what* data is relevant. Today information organizes itself via search engine. And our culture, with its access to media, expects excellence. Young adults experience the highest quality of Christianity on their monitors, in their iPods, and on their flat screens.

College students can download sermons from Alistair Begg and Billy Graham, among the world's other well-known preachers. The megachurch down the road has some of the highest quality music in the region, Christian or secular. Christian resource companies make available some of the best study material ever created. Some churches pipe live feeds of their nationally known pastor into remote sites via video screen. How can churches, small-group leaders, and pastors *compete* with all of the high quality media available?

We're not competing.

Our research revealed an amazing fact: the younger generation is not leaving their church to attend a bigger, brighter, fancier, snazzier, louder, and hipper congregation. They may end up attending these churches, but it is not because the megachurch is pulling them into their attractive gravitational field. In fact, in all three parts of our research, we heard almost nothing from teens and young adults desiring to go to a high-impact, high-quality megachurch. Of all the major reasons eighteen- to twenty-two-year-olds leave their church, a lack of polish was not one of them.

In our conversations with pastors and leaders in the church, we hear the retorts.

"We just don't have the capabilities to do what the big church across town does."

"We just don't have the talent to put on a worship service like them."

"I'm not as good a communicator as their pastor."

These worries and arguments are unfounded. The younger generation does not leave their church because of a desire to attend a higher quality worship service. We have no doubt that churches, small or large, that create an atmosphere of excellence do *attract* people. But other churches in the area are not declining as a *result* of another church's excellence. Students leave churches because of inadequacies and unhealthiness within their churches, not because another church is healthier, bigger, and better.

Having other healthy churches in the area can only help your church. The healthier the universal body of believers, the healthier a local church can become. The goal of leaders is not to compete with other churches in the vicinity. The goal of the pastor and other leaders is to get students to buy into their church despite the foibles. Sam didn't lose any members after puking into a live mike during the Sunday morning worship. In fact, most of the students in the church got a grand laugh out of it. One of the college students even helped clean up the mess!

Students crave leaders who are transparent. They seek leaders who will admit mistakes. Excellence is important. Putting the work and time into a sermon is critical. As we stated earlier, these students balk at poor preaching, but they aren't looking for frothy eloquence. This generation wants excellence that comes with a heavy dose of reality. They want a pastor who leads by example. Young adults look for a pastor who lives what he preaches. If the pastor says he's passionate about seeing people come to know Christ, then they'll check to see if he's doing the work of an evangelist.

Polished figureheads don't necessarily impress the younger generation. Even though he's a wonderful orator, there's a reason we don't show reruns of Billy Graham every week in our churches. There's a reason we don't pipe John Piper via satellite into every congregation on Sunday. There's a reason Internet church will never truly work. This generation wants a real shepherd, flaws and all. This generation desires a relationship with *their* pastor, the one at *their* church. He's *their* leader. Excellent pastors know the specific dynamics of *their* local church. They relate to *their* people. They engage *their* students. This involvement trumps the megachurch wow factor. It surmounts the availability of the Internet. These essential churches have essential pastors, no matter how big or small the congregation.

The platform upon which to build. Students are dropping out of churches at an alarming rate. Of those who will drop out of church, 70 percent do so between the ages of eighteen and twenty-two. We are losing an entire generation at one of the most critical junctions in their lives. They leave because of life changes. They leave because of poor leadership in the church. They leave because of a lack of authenticity. They leave because the church has not reached out to them and their peers. They leave because the church has nothing for them at their particular life stage. But the tide of those leaving can be stemmed. Churches can plug the flow of the young adult exodus. A solution exists. In the next section we will detail what our research revealed as a way to keep these young adults and begin to attract others.

While many are leaving or have left their local body, hope is still found. A platform upon which to build exists. Our research shed light on some welcoming news: two-thirds of all young adults who attended a Protestant church for at least a year in high school currently consider themselves Christian.[11] The conclusion is this generation has not abandoned their faith. They walked away from the church, which is obviously the wrong path to walk. But they remain receptive. They still relate to their Christian roots.

Churches can reclaim this generation. In order for this mass of students to return, however, the church must demonstrate that it is essential to their lives. Our local churches must begin to shift the focus back on to the younger generation. We've got to meet them where they are. And we must prove to them that a biblically sound body of believers is essential to the lives of every Christian, young and old alike.

PART 2

How Essential
Churches Close the
Back Door

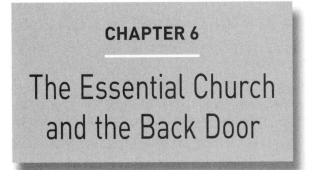

CHAPTER 6

The Essential Church and the Back Door

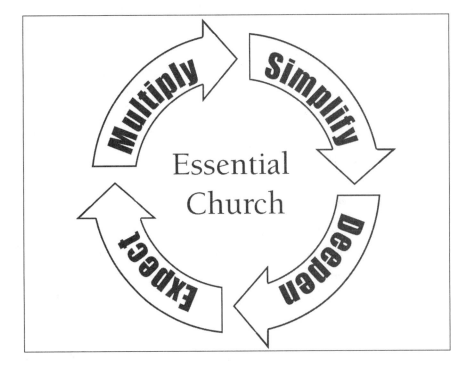

OK, we admit it. In this book we've shared many negative stories. We have told you what's wrong with the American church, and we've given you the research and the statistics to support our gloomy thesis. We are not pessimists. To the contrary, despite the evidence that suggests otherwise, we are obnoxious optimists.

We have two reasons for our seemingly unfounded optimism. First, we don't think God is done with us yet. We have seen too many indicators that He is working in obvious ways in many churches across America. Second, we have heard from two groups of people who give us further hope. One group represents those who never left the church. These churched Americans have some incredible stories about what is right with many churches. We will hear from them shortly. The second group includes those people who left the church and subsequently returned. They are the rechurched, and they have their own amazing stories.

One purpose of this book, stated simply, is to share how churches can retain those who are already attending and to reveal how churches can reach those who left the church. Such is the essential church. And in this second section of the book we move from descriptive to prescriptive. We believe the stories and research of people who have been positively impacted by essential churches are worth telling.

Denzel: A Success Story of the Churched

Denzel became a Christian at the age of fourteen. His parents had never attended church until he was ten years old. Then his father was told that he had cancer and that he probably would not survive a year. But Denzel's dad not only survived; he has been cancer-free for ten years.

His dad's close brush with death led Denzel's parents to seek greater meaning in their lives. They began attending Forest Glen Community Church, and they have never looked back. Both parents became followers of Christ, and young Denzel followed a few years later.

Unlike the majority of his peers, Denzel never dropped out of church. To the contrary, he will graduate from college in two years, and he has remained as active in his church at age twenty as he was at age ten.

"I actually chose a college close to home so I could stay active at Forest Glen," Denzel told us. "I learned at an early age how essential church is to my life, and I plan on remaining active as long as God gives me the ability to serve."

He said it.

Denzel said those words that reflect the summation of all those interviews we conducted: "I learned at an early age how *essential church* is to my life." Of course, this singular statement did more than pique our curiosity. It led us to an in-depth interview to hear how a church became essential to one person.

"Even at the age of ten," Denzel began, "I could understand what Forest Glen was all about. They said it over and over: 'Connect to God; connect to others; connect to the world.' I heard Pastor Mike say those words almost every week when he was preaching or making announcements. Almost all of my Sunday school teachers talked about it. Even before I was a Christian, I had a clear idea what the church was all about."

When Denzel became a Christian, he was required to attend a new Christian's class and a new member's class for youth. "They made the classes fun, but they were serious as well," he recalled. "At the time I thought all churches were like Forest Glen," he laughed. "But later I found that we were somewhat of an exception."

"How did you become a Christian?"

Denzel smiled at that question. "Our church is infused with the Great Commission. You can't be in the church two weeks without some type of evangelistic encounter. I guess I'm kind of surprised that it took me four years to become a Christian.

Not only did I become a Christian; I was taught the importance of the Great Commission for my own life. I feel well equipped to share my own faith, and I have been on four overseas mission trips and one mission trip to New Orleans."

What else could Denzel share with us about Forest Glen Community Church? "Well, the church is serious about teaching the Word," he began. "They systematically teach the whole Bible at the elementary age and then repeat the process at a higher level for those in middle school and high school. Now that I am at the young adult level, I have the opportunity to study the Bible even deeper in Sunday school and small groups."

Denzel did not stop there. "The preaching is meaty," he began. "It's not that Pastor Mike preaches and teaches above our heads; it's that we get solid biblical teaching every week. I really look forward to church because I learn so much. I've heard some people say that deep preaching and teaching can't be relevant. I totally disagree. Not only do we learn biblical truths at Forest Glen, but we also learn how those truths apply to our lives."

Denzel is a classic example of the thesis of this book. He has remained a faithful member and attendee of Forest Glen Community Church because he sees the church as essential to his life. Review some of his comments:

> *Simplify: The Right Structure.* "Even at the age of ten, I could understand what Forest Glen was all about. They said it over and over: 'Connect to God; connect to others; connect to the world.'"

> *Deepen: The Right Content.* "The preaching is meaty. It's not that Pastor Mike preaches and teaches above our heads; it's that we get solid biblical teaching every week. I've heard some people say that deep preaching and teaching can't be relevant. I totally disagree. Not only do we learn biblical truths at Forest Glen, but we also learn how those truths apply to our lives."

Expect: The Right Attitude. When Denzel became a Christian, he was required to attend a new Christian's class and a new member's class for youth. "They made the classes fun, but they were serious as well," he recalled. "At the time I thought all churches were like Forest Glen," he laughed. "But later I found that we were somewhat of an exception."

Multiply: The Right Action. "I was taught the importance of the Great Commission for my own life. I feel well equipped to share my own faith, and I have been on four overseas mission trips and one mission trip to New Orleans."

Denzel represents well those young adults who made it through adolescence and youth without leaving the church. Church is essential to their lives, and they do not view their congregations as an optional activity. But, if two-thirds of these young people leave the church, how can we get them back? Rhonda's story is telling.

Rhonda: From Dechurched to Rechurched

"I was born in the church," Rhonda laughed. "My parents were charter members of Highland Avenue Baptist Church, and they got me in the nursery just six weeks after I was born. I was at church three or four times a week until I got my driver's license. After that I attended less frequently. By the time I left home to go to college, I was a total church dropout."

Rhonda's story is incredibly similar to so many of the young dropouts we interviewed. Do you remember the point of the "unsweet sixteen"? The church's struggle to retain young people reaches a critical point when they turn age sixteen, the time when Rhonda got her driver's license. By the time the teen reaches between seventeen and nineteen, the dropout rate peaks.[1]

Percentage gain/loss for age categories in the church	
Between 15 and 16	+1%
Between 16 and 17	-15%
Between 17 and 18	-24%
Between 18 and 19	-29%
Between 19 and 20	-5%

Rhonda's story matches these numbers well. By the time she left home for college, she was "a total church dropout." Indeed, the largest numbers of dropouts take place at that decisive age between eighteen and nineteen, whether they attend college or not.

Rhonda's story does not end there. Rhonda is now active in another church. She is among the rechurched in America. What happened? In just a few short years, how did one woman move from churched to dechurched to rechurched? At this point her story will probably not surprise you.

"I never was really mad at the church," she began. "I just became less and less active, and no one seemed to notice. By the time I left for college, church was no longer a vital part of my life. But I always thought I would return one day."

Rhonda's new job out of college moved her to Southern California. She met a man whom she dated for several months. He then proposed, and the wedding date was set.

"I was so happy," she recalled. "And then my world crashed."

For Rhonda the crash was the breakup with her fiancé. "It was so unexpected," she said softly. "One day we were making wedding plans, and the next day he said he couldn't go through with it. It was really bizarre. I never saw him again. I don't know if it was a bad case of cold feet or he found someone else. I just knew that I was deeply hurt."

Natalie is a coworker and friend of Rhonda's. They had spent a lot of time together, so Natalie knew a lot about her friend. "Natalie was so perceptive," Rhonda told us. "She is really a strong Christian. She invited me to church when we first met, but she didn't push. When my engagement fell apart, she asked if she could pray for me. I realized how much I missed being around Christian friends so I starting going to church with Natalie."

Rhonda began to describe the church. "Franklin Road Community Church is absolutely incredible. The people are like Natalie, caring and outwardly focused. The preaching is relevant and deeply biblical. I always sense the presence of God in the worship services. I am in the process of going through an informative membership class where they repeatedly teach about their discipleship process. The church is one of the most evangelistic churches I have ever attended. They expect every member to be involved in some type of ministry to people outside the church."

We could continue sharing Rhonda's effusive testimony about Franklin Road Community Church, but we are sure you get the point by now. Rhonda dropped out of a nonessential church, but she returned to an essential church.

I guess we should mention one more personal aspect of Rhonda's story. She met Craig at the church. By the time you read this book, they will be married.

Building the Essential Church

With the plethora of statistics and surveys we shared with you, we know that some of you may feel like your head is spinning. I (Thom) have written a number of books on the church. Most of them, like this book, are based on objective research. When Sam and I began work on this project, we were determined to provide solid research, but we wanted more. We wanted to be able to share not only descriptive data; we wanted to provide some prescriptive solutions. That is our goal in this second section of the book.

Some caveats are in order. First, by its very nature, prescription is subjective. But we do have the research data to back our suggestions. We also have the experience of hundreds of church consultations to reinforce our recommended pathways.

Second, some of the prescriptions go beyond the survey research of the young dropouts. Those prescriptions are formed by previous research by Thom, much of which has been published in earlier books.[2] In some ways this section, though specifically focusing on the crisis of young dropouts, is really the culmination of more than two decades of research and consultation with churches across America.

Fleshing Out the Structure

In the next chapter we will talk about the simple structure needed for effective discipleship in the local church. But the remainder of the book answers the questions, *What now?* Now that we know what the structure should look like, where do we go next? As we have indicated earlier, we believe the essential church focuses on four major issues: simplify, deepen, expect, and multiply. We will devote a chapter to each of these issues, but let's see how they relate specifically to the research of the young dropouts.

The Problem of Complexity Instead of Simplicity

By this point we have made abundantly clear that the church's structure, its process of discipleship, is by no means the most important aspect of the church. But we have also indicated that complex, weak, or bad structures can become impediments to the church in its most important functions.

What indicators in our research led us to believe that a complex structure was a contributor to the dropout rate? The evidence seems clear that this issue was a major problem.

The dropouts did not feel connected with people in the church. One of every five dropouts indicated that they had no meaningful relationships with other members of the church. That is a clear sign of poor structure. A healthy structure, such as the simple church we discuss in the next chapter, is designed with intentionality to move members into small groups, Sunday school classes, and ministry groups. In the context of those groups, relationships are formed.

In my (Thom's) earlier research on the effectiveness of Sunday school classes as an assimilation approach, I found that those in a Sunday school class were much more likely to remain active in a church than those who attended worship services only.[3] Though I did not conduct identical studies on the assimilation effectiveness of other small groups, the anecdotal evidence is overwhelming. People stick with churches where they have healthy interpersonal relationships, and those relationships often form in the context of small groups.

The structural problem in many churches is that people are not intentionally led toward small groups, and thus relationships are not formed. Though this problem spans the generations, it is especially acute among teenagers where healthy relationships are vital.

The dropouts feel more connected with people outside the church. "I dropped out of church when I started hanging out with some drinking buddies." John's statement was straightforward and stated with little apparent emotion. At age seventeen, John formed his closest relationships with other underage alcohol drinkers. That social group replaced his social group at church.

"Yeah, I did have some friends at church, but I was not that close to them when I got to middle and high school. In my elementary school years, Sunday school was a big part of my life, but it was not pushed as much for the teenagers. My church emphasized big events for youth. They were fun, but it was hard to connect with people. I'm not sure how I ended up with my drinking buddies, but they became my best friends."

John is now twenty-eight years old, and three of his closest friends today are still the drinking buddies from his teen years. For many of the dropouts we interviewed, their social networks formed with a teenage version of the old sitcom *Cheers*, "where everybody knows your name."

One of five dropouts (20 percent) indicated that they did not feel connected with people in their former churches. A similar number (17 percent) told us that other social groups outside the church replaced their church fellowship.

Humans by nature are social creatures. We will find social relationships one way or the other. The tragedy here is that these dechurched persons that we interviewed had been active in the church, on the average, for many years but they left because they felt disconnected. The church did not meet their needs of genuine fellowship.

The first church is described vividly in Acts 2:42–47.

> *And they devoted themselves to the apostles' teaching, to fellowship, to the breaking of bread, and to prayers.*
>
> *Then fear came over everyone, and many wonders and signs were being performed through the apostles. Now all the believers were together and had everything in common. So they sold their possessions and property and distributed the proceeds to all, as anyone had a need. And every day they devoted themselves to meeting together in the temple complex, and broke bread from house to house. They ate their food with gladness and simplicity of heart, praising God and having favor with all the people. And every day the Lord added to them those who were being saved.*

Among the many fascinating aspects of this passage is the emphasis on fellowship, the Greek word *koinonia*. Luke tells us in these verses that the early followers of the risen Savior first dedicated themselves to the teachings, or the content of the faith, and then to fellowship with one another.

The early church exemplifies for the church of the twenty-first century that the congregation must bond in true Christian fellowship. We doubt that anyone who reads this book will challenge us on that issue. And most Christians who are active in churches will tell us that fellowship in their churches with friends whom they know and love is one of the primary reasons they are involved in their churches.

Let's stop for a moment and do a ruthless assessment of our churches. If a guest came into our church with no previous relational connections, how difficult would it be for him or her to connect with others? We have to take off the blinders that we have because we have long-term church relationships. Can we honestly say that an outsider could come into our church and quickly develop meaningful friendships with other members?

We have been asking new members and guests of churches that question for over a decade. And the reality is that the contrast in perceptions between new members and longer term members is often stark. The longer term members see their church as friendly and connecting, but the newer members often see the church as cliquish and only superficially friendly.

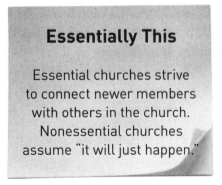

Essentially This

Essential churches strive to connect newer members with others in the church. Nonessential churches assume "it will just happen."

A complex church will have a plethora of activities. A complex church will have many organizations and programs. But a complex church is typically weak at intentionally bringing members into meaningful Christian relationships with one another. Frankly, these churches are just too busy at activities to be intentional at most anything except maintaining their activities.

Lack of intentionality in connecting people is just one of the problems of a complex church. A number of the dropouts left the church because they did not feel they were growing spiritually in the church. Let's take a brief look at that issue.

Some of the dropouts did not feel that the church was helping them to develop spiritually. We were impressed with the honesty of the dechurched we interviewed. For the most part they did not have a victim mentality. They took much of the responsibility for their spiritual detours. Still, they did not hesitate to let us know that the church could have done a better job.

One of seven dropouts shared that the church was not conducive to his or her spiritual growth. We would have loved to dig deeper into this response, but we are able to isolate a few causes. And one of those causes takes us right back to complexity. The church was busy with activities, but it did not have a clear process of disciple making. Listen to Sherry's story.

"I joined the church initially because of the great worship service. I always felt the presence of God in those times," she reflected. "I never studied the Bible that much, and I did not really know how to grow as a Christian. So I went to one of the pastors, and he recommended that I get involved in some particular programs and groups at the church."

Sherry continued, "The programs I got involved in were great, but I still didn't get it. I didn't understand how they connected. I even asked my pastor if the church's plan for helping Christians grow spiritually was getting us busy in a bunch of disconnected activities. I don't think he appreciated my question."

Sherry dropped out of church for three years. But she eventually found a church whose process for disciple making was clear and expected. "It's so common sense," she told us. "Just let us know how we can become more mature spiritually. It probably won't be a perfect process, but it will be better than the churches that have no process of discipleship at all."

The Problem with Shallowness Instead of Depth

In my twenty-plus years of consulting with churches, I (Thom) have heard similar statements so many times that I have lost count:

> "Our church focuses on discipleship instead of evangelism. We leave the evangelistic activities to others."

> "We consider ourselves to be Great Commission evangelists at our church, so we don't spend much time on discipleship."

> "At our church we focus on healthy fellowship. Other churches are called to do evangelism or discipleship, but our calling is different."

Of course, you can see the absurdity of these comments. Nowhere in the New Testament do we find "specialist" churches. All churches are called to be evangelistic, to make disciples, to have God-glorifying worship, to be people of prayer, and to have healthy Christian fellowship.

At least anecdotally, it seems that the most frequently mentioned dichotomy is between evangelism and discipleship. Church leaders often boast that their churches focus on one at the expense of the other. A true New Testament church must be evangelistic. A true New Testament church must be about the business of disciple making. The balance is not an option but a mandate.

A number of the dechurched admitted that they were biblically ignorant. They confessed that they only had a shallow knowledge of biblical doctrines. And while they usually took personal responsibility for their lack of biblical understanding, they also blamed many of the churches for the doctrinal ignorance. Look at some of the responses that are closely related to this issue. Though the percentage is not high for any one response, the cumulative impact is undeniable.

> *The church was not helping me to develop spiritually*
> *(13 percent).* We related this issue above as a possible
> problem with complexity, but it could be that
> the church was simply not providing spiritual and
> doctrinal training.

> *I disagreed with the church's moral and ethical guidelines*
> *for everyday living (16 percent).* Obviously many
> churches are not tying moral and ethical issues to
> biblical truth.

> *I disagreed with the church's teaching about God*
> *(14 percent).* If the church could not support basic
> teachings about God biblically, we wonder what was
> being taught.

> *I was unsure of the reasons behind my faith (13 percent).*
> Again, basic biblical training seems conspicuously
> absent in many of the churches.

More than half of the church dropouts (52 percent) left the church because of differences or uncertainty about the church's religious, ethical, or political beliefs. At least part of this problem can be directly attributed to shallow biblical teaching and preaching in the church. One dechurched respondent indicated that the doctrinal teaching at his former church was "piecemeal Christianity."

"I would hear about passages from three or four books of the Bible in a single sermon, but I couldn't figure out how they tied together," Marcus told us. "And then I would go to a small group, and we would talk about some great issues, but no one explained how it tied in to the totality of Scripture. I felt so embarrassed about not knowing where the books of the Bible were located that I taught myself. After four years at that church, I had not received any significant doctrinal teachings. I can't blame anyone but myself for not being in some church, but I can blame the shallow teachings of my former church for at least part of the reason I left."

We will look at this issue of "deepen" more fully in chapter 8. But the young people are, for the most part, bright and eager to learn. We do them a great disservice by failing to challenge them and instruct them in the depths of God's Word.

The Problem with Low Expectations Instead of High Expectations

When I (Thom) was a pastor in St. Petersburg, Florida, my wife and I had three young sons. Sam, the coauthor of this book, was the oldest at eight years old. I love the climate of that coastal city. In fact, we celebrated our first Christmas there by going swimming in the Gulf of Mexico. The year-round warmth and sunshine was great for all of us.

There were times, however, when loading up the kids to travel the short ten-minute trip to the ocean was not the preference of the boys. They wanted to go to a swimming pool. The problem was that we did not have a swimming pool. We did not have membership in a club that had a pool. And we could only intrude on our pool-blessed neighbors when we were invited.

"Thom," my wife Nellie Jo informed me, "the Elks' lodge has a swimming pool. And we could walk there from our house."

"But I'm not an Elk," I objected.

Nellie Jo gave me the look.

I became an Elk.

I rationalized that I could pay a minimum fee and stay minimally involved and the family could have the year-round convenience of a nearby pool.

Not so.

The requirements for membership were clear. The expectations were not low. In fact, I still have my old membership card that says, "A good Elk is an active Elk." I had to become an active Elk. My family got the swimming pool.

My point? The expectations of civic organizations are typically higher than those of the church. In many of our churches, membership means filling out a card, walking an aisle, or, in some tough cases, attending a membership class. Then you can go incognito. You can fall through the cracks and not be noticed.

In the introductory chapter of this book, you met Travis. He was the big guy with the earrings. He had been active in church all of his life until he dropped out as a teenager. And no one noticed. No one contacted him. No one seemed to care. He apparently is still on the membership roll of the church, but no one has declared him AWOL.

As we stated earlier, our purpose in this second half of the book is to provide possible solutions to the dropout problem. One issue is clear. We aren't seeing much commitment from many church members because we are expecting so little from them. Let's review some of the other reasons the dechurched left their churches:

I simply wanted a break from church. This reason was the number one reason for the departure from church for the eighteen- to twenty-two-year-olds. They wanted a break. More than one-fourth (27 percent) gave this reason to explain why they left the church. They just wanted a break.

Can you imagine what would have happened if a student in high school just stopped attending school because he or she just wanted a break? OK, we realize that school dropouts are a reality, but our society recognizes it as a serious problem. We exhort students to stay in school. States enact laws that prohibit school dropouts before a certain age. We declare that it is a problem that needs our full attention. Even if a relatively small number do actually drop out, we still look at any level of school dropouts as a potential problem.

But church dropouts?

Oh well.

Let us pick on our denomination for a moment. The Southern Baptist Convention claims more than sixteen million members on our inflated church rolls. But on a given Sunday, only six to seven million are in attendance. We probably have five or six million members who never show up, or their attendance pattern is CEO (Christmas, Easter, and Other special events).

We do have some in our denomination who are recognizing the crisis for what it is, but most of us don't lose sleep over the lost sheep.

Oh well.

I (Sam) pastored a church that had four times as many on the membership roll than could be found. We slowly and carefully addressed the issue. But where did these members go?

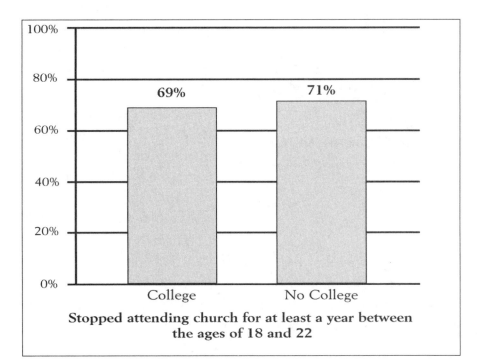

Stopped attending church for at least a year between the ages of 18 and 22

We expect little, and we receive little. Church membership does not matter because we have such low expectations of our members. Need a break from the church? No problem. Come back in a few years if you can.

I moved to college and stopped attending church. One fourth (25 percent) of the dropouts cited this explanation. As we discussed earlier, we can't blame the colleges and universities for the dropouts. The number of dropouts is statistically the same whether they went to college or not.

The bottom line is that during the critical transition after high school graduation, these young adults no longer saw church as essential to their lives. Frankly, most churches never put forth expectations of the students in their ministries. The church leaders may have made available to them Sunday school classes or small groups. They may have offered ministry opportunities and mission trips. They may have provided great entertainment and some meaningful worship experiences.

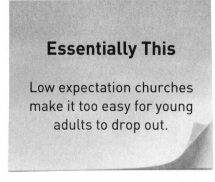

Essentially This

Low expectation churches make it too easy for young adults to drop out.

But most church leaders and parents never communicated lovingly that church is a vital part of their lives. They rarely shared with them the expectation that they should be involved in ministry in church life, not just attending functions.

Most young adults will seek employment. Why? It is expected of them.

Most young adults will complete a level of education. Why? It is expected of them.

Most young adults will remain loyal to friends and social networks. Why? It is expected of them.

But more than two-thirds of young adults will drop out of church before their twenty-second birthday. Why? Church was an option. Church existed to serve them. In most cases serving others through the church was never an expectation.

And if you don't expect a behavior, you are unlikely to get it.

The Problem with an Inward Focus Instead of Multiplication

Luke states it as a fact in Acts 2:47: "And every day the Lord added to them those who were being saved." He makes it seem that evangelism was just a natural part of the New Testament church.

Why? Because it was.

The church that is not multiplying, not reaching people, not starting new churches, and not involved in missions is the New Testament anomaly. Unfortunately we have a lot of anomalies among our churches today.

Let us be blunt if we have not already done so to this point. Many of our churches are producing a lot of soft and self-centered Christians. And the young people in our churches are getting the message. Through the actions of many of our church leaders, they are hearing that the church is all about them, that the church is there to serve them, and that the church is the place for all their needs and desires to be met.

Churches that are outwardly focused are sending a different message: The church is not all about my needs; it's about how I can glorify God as I meet the needs of others. That is the irony of the essential church. The outwardly focused church creates better inwardly focused assimilation. As our young people meet the needs of others, they see that they are important to the life of the church, and thus they are prone not to enter the ranks of the dechurched.

Listen again to the aggregate responses of the dechurched, as we add emphases at obvious points:

I simply wanted a break from church (27 percent).
I became too busy (22 percent).
School responsibilities prevented *me* from attending
    church (16 percent).
Church was not helping *me* to develop spiritually
    (13 percent).
Church did not offer programs of interest to *me*
    (11 percent).

The list could continue, but the point is made. For many of the young people in the church, it was all about them. And we are not placing all of the blame on the young adults who left. While there does seem to be self-centered motivations in dropping out of church, we know that many churches communicate that message of self-centeredness. But the essential church looks beyond its own walls.

Certainly the church should be concerned about the members who comprise the body. But if those members are never expected to evangelize or to be on the mission field, the church has turned inward. And the consequence is not only neglected fields of harvest; the members themselves turn into soft Christians, more concerned about their needs than those of the hurting world around them. Such Christians will soon feel unneeded or even unwanted in the church. They then become prime candidates to enter the world of the dechurched.

The Problem and a Possible Solution

We two Rainers have not hesitated to describe the problems of the church, particularly the American church. We have given you a plethora of dizzying facts and statistics that probably understate the woeful condition of most churches. We have spent most of this book focusing on those who drop out between the ages of eighteen and twenty-two because that is the time when we are most likely to lose members. That is the time when the back door is wide open.

We are not satisfied to provide the description of gloom, as accurate as it may be. We want to be a part of the solution. And we still believe in the God of miracles. The hard facts do not diminish our hope.

There is a danger, however, in offering solutions. One of those dangers is for the solution to be formulaic: "If we just do A, B, and C, our church will be healthy, and we can close the back door."

Our proposed solutions are neither formulaic nor easy. To the contrary, they require much work and much commitment. The faint of heart and the lackadaisical Christians should not move in this direction. Much work needs to be done.

Another danger is that some may see our solutions to be methods without God. That is what a formula is anyway. The easy ABC approach is man centered and not God centered.

We thus offer these proposed paths with fear and trembling before a sovereign God. They should not be entered into lightly or unadvisedly but prayerfully and fearfully before God. Indeed, we would encourage any church leader to go into a season of prayer before tackling any change, much less major change in a church.

Still, our proposals are not taken out of thin air. We are reporting in summary form the paths of some of the healthiest churches in our nation. We are sharing with you what some churches do well. These are the churches that are not seeing the mass exodus of young people between the ages of eighteen and twenty-two. These are the churches that are reaching them and keeping them.

As we report these solutions to you, we will note along the way how a positive approach responds to many of the reasons the young people left the church. And as you can guess by now, all of these paths are about the essential church, churches that are essential to the lives of those in the church and thus are essential to those on the outside they are trying to reach in God's power.

At the risk of redundancy, we share again what these churches have in common:

1. They have *simplified* their structures so that a path of discipleship is clear.
2. They provide rich and *deep* biblical teachings.
3. They raised the level of *expectations* of the members of the church.
4. They are on mission to *multiply* through evangelism and other outwardly focused ministries.

Such is the essential church. Now let's find out how our churches can keep the young people who are prone to exit. And let's find out how, in the process, the totality of our churches' health improves.

We begin with the simplification of the church structure. We call it the simple church.

CHAPTER 7

Simplify: Getting the Structure Right

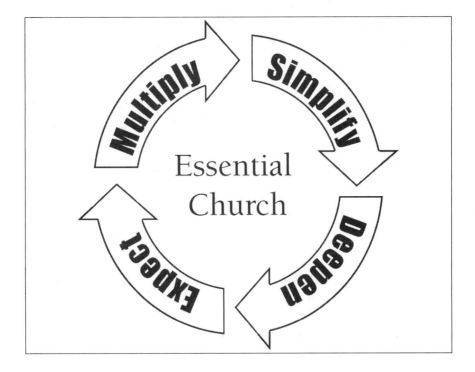

Our conversation with Rachel was revealing. She could have contributed to almost every top-ten item on why people left the church. Do you remember that top-ten list?

Top Ten Reasons Church Dropouts Stopped Attending Church

1. Simply wanted a break from church.
2. Church members seemed judgmental or hypocritical.
3. Moved to college and stopped attending church.
4. Work responsibilities prevented me from attending.
5. Moved too far away from the church to continue attending.
6. Became too busy, though still wanted to attend.
7. Didn't feel connected to the people in my church.
8. Disagreed with the church's stance on political or social issues.
9. Chose to spend more time with friends outside the church.
10. Was only going to church to please others.

"You know, I think I was really only going to church to please my parents [10]," she began. "I really needed a break from church to think for myself [1], and when I moved to Gainesville to go to college, I thought it would be a good time to evaluate things [3 and 5]. But when I graduated from college and moved to Chicago, I just became too busy at work to think about church [6]. And I just got tired of my church back home where the members seemed so hypocritical [2], and where many of them were more concerned about their pet issues than true Christianity [8]."

Wow. Seven of ten in one response. We might have hit all ten reasons if the interview had lasted longer.

This time, in our interview with Rachel, we asked her a hypothetical question: "What would you do if you knew you had to start attending a church regularly within a week? In other words, all excuses are off the table."

Her hesitation was brief, and her honesty was compelling. "I would be scared," she said emphatically. "I have visited a few churches in the area, but I refused to get involved because you have to know all the rules to understand what is going on."

We were not clear about these "rules," so we asked her to clarify. "I went to my church at home for eleven years. I learned over time all the programs and activities. I learned what I was supposed to do and not supposed to do. But the only way I learned was by being raised in that church and by being exposed to all the activities and unwritten rules over the years."

Then Rachel made a statement that summed it up well: "Churches today are just too confusing." Then her eyes grew wide and she grinned broadly. "I would like to see older long-term church members try to get involved in a new church. Let's see how comfortable they would be in these complicated churches."

The Simple Church

Once all the excuses are removed, once the dechurched have the strong desire to return to church, and once the first steps are made, it is still difficult for these church dropouts to return to church. And this time the problem is not with the dechurched; the problem resides with the church. Rachel is right. Churches have become too complicated, and the unwanted barriers to entry (or reentry) are many.

Eric Geiger and Thom coauthored a book called *Simple Church*.[1] It became a best seller as it seemed to hit a nerve in the church in America. From the pastor to the nominal church member, there is a sense that church has become too complicated and too busy. There is no clear path for someone to grow as a disciple. Instead of a cogent path of discipleship, churches offer a series of seemingly unconnected programs and activities. We heard in the previous chapters how many young people left the church because they were never truly discipled. They may have been involved in a plethora of activities, but they weren't discipled.

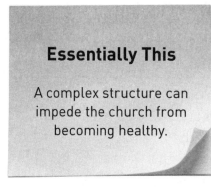

Essentially This

A complex structure can impede the church from becoming healthy.

Here is the essence of how our research connected to the simple church. Without a clear and cogent structure such as that depicted in *Simple Church*, the other three facets of the essential church are rendered meaningless.

Doctrine and biblical depth *(Deepen)* are more important than a simple structure. But most churches do not have a structure in place that readily moves people toward an understanding of doctrine and biblical depth so it never happens in their lives.

High expectations *(Expect)* in churches are more important than a simple structure. But most churches do not have structure in place that readily moves people toward an understanding of those expectations.

Evangelism and church multiplication *(Multiply)* are more important than a simple structure. But most churches do not have structures in place that readily move people toward a greater Great Commission heart and action.

Do you get the picture?

The right structure is not the most important facet of a church, but most churches cannot carry out their most important purposes because they do not have the right structure.

The Simple Steps of the Simple Church

OK, simplifying the church is not that simple. Eric Geiger and Thom have received hundreds of e-mails from church leaders have followed the insights of *Simple Church* and have raved about the new life that has been breathed into their churches. But it was not always easy. Changing direction can be difficult and sometimes painful. That is why both Eric and Thom urged the leaders to move carefully. Those who did so were blessed immeasurably according to their own testimonies.

But the concept of a simple church is, well, simple.

We encourage you to read *Simple Church* if you have not already done so. But for those of you who will not get around to reading the book, allow us to give you its essence while relating it to the essential church. First, here is the definition of a simple church: *A simple church is a congregation designed around a straightforward and strategic process that moves people through the stages of spiritual growth.* The simple church has four major components: clarity, movement, alignment, and focus. Where these four elements are missing, the dechurched often have an unsuccessful reentry into the church, and it's part of the reason they left. Let's look at each of these facets individually.

The Simple Church, Step 1: Clarity

Frankly, most of the young-adult dechurched that we interviewed in our study became confused when they attempted reentry into a church. And they were confused even when they were active in a church. They were uncertain what the church was all about; they did not know the church's purpose. And this generation, as we noted earlier, is not their parent's generation. They do not attend church just because they are supposed to attend church. There must be a purpose behind their actions.

Can you imagine interviewing for a job with, say, Microsoft, and you asked the interviewer what Microsoft did? And what if in their response, instead of giving you a clear understanding of what the company did, they began to tell you about their different divisions, departments, and activities. You then repeat the question, but the interviewer again tells you some of the activities of the eighty thousand employees. You would probably leave the interview shaking your head. You just wanted to know what the company did.

You would be expecting a straightforward response like: "Microsoft develops, manufactures, licenses, and supports a wide range of software products for computing devices." Then you would get it. You could now make an informed decision about joining the company if they offered you a job.

How much more important, then, is it for the local church to be clear about its purpose? Unfortunately most churches in America look like a web of somewhat related activities that have no clear goal in mind. The young dechurched today, if they are to return to church, must see a clear and compelling purpose in the church they ultimately may choose. And they may not ever become dropouts if the church has that clear and compelling purpose.

Clarity should essentially have two components: *what* and *how*. What is the purpose of the church? How will that purpose be accomplished?

In *Simple Church* Thom and Eric used the example of Cross Church. The leaders of that church decided that they wanted to be explicitly clear on the purpose of the church. They knew that they would be less effective in reaching either the unchurched or the dechurched without a clear purpose. In fact, they knew that their own members needed a clear path of discipleship.

Their first decision in the step of clarity was to determine what they hoped God would do to transform the members of the church. Cross Church leaders decided that disciples at their church would be passionate lovers of God, servants in the kingdom of God, and connected in vibrant relationships to people.

But the leaders of the church knew that they could not stop there. The goal is lofty and well intended, but it had no means for it to be carried out. So the leaders took the next step and described this purpose as a process. This process definition is much easier to grasp if the leaders describe their church purpose statement as a process.

Cross Church then took their desire for disciples and placed them in sequential order: "Love God. Love others. Serve the world." Someone first commits to love God. The person then gets connected in vibrant relationships with others and finally expresses love for God and for others by serving the world.

The leaders at Cross Church believe that spiritual growth is a process, and they described the focus of their church in such terms. The order is important. It provides a clear blueprint for the leaders at the church.

The purpose statement of Cross Church is good: "Love God. Love others. Serve the world." It describes not only what the goal is but also how the goal will be accomplished. But let's be honest. The programs and ministries are what people see. People forget the statements on the wall no matter how many times leaders exhort them to memorize them. But the people in the church do understand the programs and ministries the church offers. The church's programs say what is important; therefore you must define how each program is used to produce the kinds of disciples God has called you to make.

The programs and ministries thus must specifically define how they will be used to move the people through the process of spiritual formation. At Cross Church, we might see the following connections:

> *Love God.* Every member of Cross Church is expected to be a regular participant in the worship services where they will draw closer to God.

> *Love others.* The people of Cross Church should be involved in a Sunday school class and/or a small group so they will be connected to others in the church.

> *Serve the world.* Cross Church has numerous ministry opportunities to serve others. Members should be involved in at least one of these offerings.

Now the picture is clearer for both the church member and the dechurched considering returning to church. Cross Church has clarified its purpose. The church has stated its purpose as a process of discipleship. And it shows how the various ministries and programs fit into this overall purpose. Clarity is thus achieved.

Lest our research become viewed as false advertising, let us be clear. Achieving clarity as the first step is work. Since *Simple Church* was published, Thom and Eric have heard from some leaders who saw the book as another quick fix, another church model to implement for their struggling congregations. Though we urged and exhorted leaders not to see the simple church in this light, some still did so to their disappointment.

The first step of simplicity, clarity, is not itself an easy step. If the church is to have a simple structure, events and activities cannot just happen. The process or purpose statement cannot be just another statement on a wall or in a drawer. If the process is to achieve clarity, it must be a regular point of discussion in the church and among the leaders.

For the simple process of clarity to become a part of the culture of the church, it first must be woven into the leadership culture. The dechurched must know within one visit of a church that the leaders are passionate about the process. If the hearts of the leaders do not beat passionately for it, the people will miss it. If the ministry blueprint is fuzzy to the leaders, it is not even thought about by the young members in the church, much less the dechurched who might be considering returning to church.

If the church is going to be simple, the process must be clear. If the process is going to be clear, then it must get into the very fabric of the church. It must become part of the character of the church. It must be foundational to the church culture. It must be in the DNA of the church's identity.

For the simple process to become woven into the identity of the church, it must be discussed frequently, not just during the early and exciting days of going simple. Clarity is not achieved without consistency.

It is not enough to unveil a vision for the *how* and then bury it among other things. It is insufficient to preach a series on the discipleship process and then file the messages. Consistent discussion is a must.

Young people recognize a confused church when they see one. So many of the reasons they stopped attending church are at least related to the church's becoming too complex. And the simple church can eliminate the confusion. Simplicity begins with clarity, but it does not end there. The second important step is movement.

The Simple Church, Step 2: Movement

Thom works in Nashville. He times his commute from the southern suburb of Franklin to downtown Nashville to avoid as much rush-hour traffic as possible. He was told that Nashville traffic was bad when he took the job as president of LifeWay Christian Resources. Though the traffic is not nearly as bad as in many other cities, he still likes to avoid the congestion.

Who likes congestion anyway? Head or chest congestion is a nuisance. You can see it on the pained faces of those struggling to breathe. When you have congestion, your day seems longer than usual. Your head or your chest hurts. You don't feel like talking because you sound funny.

Congestion in the head or chest prevents movement. The movement of air is hindered because of congestion. Your head or chest is full of stuff that is not supposed to be there. Mucus, phlegm, and junk clog your body. The extra stuff prevents your sinuses from functioning properly.

Congestion is bad.

Many churches are congested.

Spiritual movement is stifled. The building of lives is slowed. And these congested churches are filled with the same people. We are not referring to the absence of new people like the young dechurched, although that is telling as well. We are referring to people staying the same. Unchanged. Unmoved.

We are talking about people not being transformed. Week after week, year after year, many people are the same. The building project of people's lives is stalled. Stagnant believers and congested churches go hand in hand.

Sadly, in many churches young people are stuck in the same place spiritually. And there is no intentional process to move them.

The young church dropouts can tell when a church is filled with spiritually stagnant members. Return with us to our conversation with Rachel. She begins to talk about the second most common reason these young people left the church ("Church members seemed judgmental or hypocritical").

"I wish I could find a church where real life change is taking place," Rachel begins. "I'm not mad at the church, but the stark hypocrisy of some church people really galls me. I don't expect people to be perfect, but I do expect to see Christians growing spiritually. I just don't see that in many churches."

The Bible paints a different picture of spiritual growth. According to Scripture a believer's life is to be transformed more and more. People are not supposed to be the same. There is to be progression, movement.

Our churches should be filled with people who are *becoming*. Becoming more like Christ. Becoming more loving and joyful. Becoming. Being transformed.

Second Corinthians 3:18 says, "We all, with unveiled faces, are reflecting the glory of the Lord and are being transformed into the same image from glory to glory; this is from the Lord who is the Spirit."

Paul is taking the reader back to Moses. Moses would walk up to this mountain called Mount Sinai. There he would meet with God face to face. It was the place where God gave Moses the Ten Commandments. Each time Moses went to meet God on this mountain, he came back glowing.

He had an encounter with God on Mount Sinai, and this encounter was so remarkable that Moses was transformed. His appearance was altered. He shone. He looked different. The first time he came down from the mountain, people were afraid. The change was that dramatic.

Moses would wear a veil over his face when he came down from the mountain. He wore a veil to cover his fading glory (2 Cor. 3:13). Once Moses left the presence of God, the glory would fade. With each step away from the mountain, the glory would decrease.

Moses had a veiled face. We have unveiled faces.

We do not have to wear a veil because the glory is not diminishing. In fact the opposite is true. The glory is ever increasing. It is so because we never leave the presence of God. We never come back down from the mountain.

The mountain is in us.

God's Spirit lives within us. We have a relationship with God that even Moses did not have. We are in the new covenant that brings righteousness, not the old covenant that brings death (2 Cor. 3:9). Moses had to go to the mountain to behold the glory of God. We don't. We have a greater level of intimacy.

Just as God transformed Moses, He transforms us when we place ourselves in His presence. The word for *transform* is in the passive voice and present tense. The passive voice indicates that we do not transform ourselves. God is the one who does the transforming. The present tense indicates that this transforming is currently taking place. Right now. As you read this. Transformation is not only a past event. God is doing a work in us right now.

The word for transformation is *metamorphosis*. It means to change the essential nature of something. It is a real change, not just a change on the outside. The core of something is changed. The word is used to describe the process a caterpillar experiences to become a butterfly. The nasty, wormy, creepy crawly insect becomes a beautiful butterfly. The process is metamorphosis.

God desires to bring His people through this morphing process. He seeks to transform the people in your church into His image. And He wants to do so with ever-increasing glory. He wants the people you serve to become more like Him tomorrow than they are today.

Congested churches and stagnant believers are the antithesis of God's plan. The simple church must first be clear about its purpose; then it must remove the congestion by helping the members toward growth. Thus movement takes place.

The essential church is a simple church, and the simple church has both clarity and movement. Like other churches, simple churches have programs, but unlike many other churches their programs are strategic. Programs fit each phase of the church's purpose and process. At Cross Church, noted earlier, the worship service helps connect people to God. The Sunday school classes and the small groups help connect people to one another. And the different ministry opportunities help people serve the world.

Simple churches not only make the movement strategic; they also make it sequential. Note that Cross Church first says to connect to a worship service, *then* connect to a Sunday school class or small group, and *then* connect to a ministry. There is a strategy to the movement, and there is a sequence to the movement.

The simple churches are intentional about helping members move toward greater maturity. Their discipleship process is simple. It is not stagnant or congested. It has movement.

Simple churches take the prescriptions. They remove the congestion. They get everyone on the same page. These are the types of churches that the young dechurched notice. But there is a third facet of the simple church. It is called alignment.

The Simple Church, Step 3: Alignment

Thom is a die-hard fan of the University of Alabama Crimson Tide. Sam graduated from the University of South Carolina. His allegiances reside with the Gamecocks, though he still has affection for his dad's team.

Thom was a student at Alabama when the legendary Paul "Bear" Bryant was football coach. The Bear coached at Alabama for twenty-five years, winning six national titles (1961, 1964, 1965, 1973, 1978, and 1979) and thirteen Southeastern Conference (SEC) championships. In other words, on average he won a national championship every four years at Alabama, and he won the SEC title every other year.

This remarkable coaching career includes another fascinating tidbit. No football player at Alabama has ever won the Heisman Trophy, college football's equivalent of the most valuable player. The Bear had a coaching philosophy that focused on the team rather than the individual. Even though he had the best teams many years while he was coach at Alabama, he resisted allowing one player to be too important. That would diminish the power of the team. That would be detrimental to the team's unity.

In the finality of Jesus' life, He was burdened for unity. In the garden He prayed that believers would be one. He said to the Father: "May they all be one, as You, Father, are in Me and I am in You. May they also be one in Us, so the world may believe You sent Me" (John 17:21).

Jesus prayed that His followers would be unified as He and the Father are. God the Father, God the Son, and God the Holy Spirit are completely one. They are inseparable. Jesus prayed that believers would be that intimate, that united, that aligned. Unity reflects the glory and character of God because God is unified.

Jesus continued, "I have given them the glory You have given Me. May they be one as We are one. I am in them and You are in Me. May they be made completely one, so the world may know You have sent Me and have loved them as You have loved Me" (John 17:22–23).

Not only does unity reflect God's character, but it also gets the attention of the world. People are attracted to unity. Young people have little patience and time for a church that is divided. They will simply move on. Jesus said that all people would know that we are His disciples by the love we have for one another (see John 13:35).

The apostle Paul encouraged the same. He challenged the church to be "thinking the same way, having the same love, sharing the same feelings, focusing on one goal" (Phil. 2:2).

Unity is powerful. It is magnetic. It is a beautiful thing. And the impact is great. Such is the essence of alignment in the simple church. Alignment is the arrangement of all ministries and staff around the simple process.

Cross Church, noted earlier in the chapter, provides an excellent example of unity. Remember the church's vision statement? "Love God. Love others. Serve the world." To promote alignment, they have fully integrated the same process into every major department in the church.

The guiding direction of the children's ministry is to lead children to love God, love others, and serve the world. The guiding direction of the youth ministry is to lead students to love God, love others, and serve the world. The vision statement for the singles' ministry is to lead young unmarried adults to love God, love others, and serve the world.

An observer of Cross Church's ministry-integrated process might say, "But that is the same thing for each area. That sounds so redundant."

Alignment is redundant in a good way.

Everyone at Cross Church understands the direction of each

ministry department. It is simple. It is the same process every-where. If you are an adult who understands the process of the adult ministry, you also understand the process of the children's ministry.

The alternative is complexity. Let's be honest. Do you really think people know the five or six different vision statements in some complex churches? Our observation is that the leaders do not even know them. Young people just ignore them. It is too complex.

Unity is promoted when the simple church is aligned. Implementing the same process everywhere prevents the church from having multiple directions. A process that is fully imple-mented pulls each ministry department together. The alternative leads to a group of subchurches that do not reflect the overall direction of the church.

"I have visited small, medium, and large churches," Rachel told us. "I really am seeking to see if I need to return to church. But all the churches I visit are downright confusing. Even the smaller churches seem to be an organization of unrelated activi-ties. Now I know one of the reasons I left the church. It just doesn't seem to make sense. If the church is only a group of loosely related activities, I can spend my time better elsewhere. I want to be somewhere that makes a difference, somewhere I can make a difference."

The complex structure of many churches is indeed an impedi-ment to the young dechurched returning to church. The complex structure is also a reason they leave the church in the first place. The alternative structure to complex is the simple church. To this point we have looked at three of the four components of the simple church:

> Clarity—a process of discipleship that can be clearly communicated and understood by the people.

> Movement—sequential steps in the process that help people to reach greater areas of commitment.

Alignment—the arrangement of the ministries,
programs, and staff around the same simple process.

Now let's look at the fourth and final component of the simple church, one that has engendered more questions to Eric and Thom than any other: focus.

Focus—the commitment to abandon those areas that
fall outside the simple ministry process.

The Simple Church, Step 4: Focus

Focus is the most difficult aspect of the simple church. Most church leaders do not want to be the guy who says no. Church leaders have feelings. Saying no is difficult because it tends to bother the person who hears it. While it may be difficult, our research indicates that it is necessary. And if you really want a structure that attracts and keeps people, the simple structure has much to commend it.

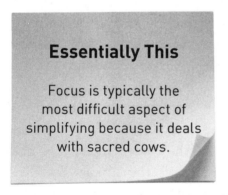

Essentially This

Focus is typically the most difficult aspect of simplifying because it deals with sacred cows.

I (Thom) serve as president of LifeWay Christian Resources, one of the largest, possibly even the largest, Christian resource companies in the world. Every day people propose ideas, projects, books, and other resources to us. We literally have thousands of ideas coming our way each year.

I actually get a few hundred of those ideas that come directly to my office. Many of them are good ideas. Everyone who proposes something to me thinks that their idea is great, and it may be. The problem I face is that I can't say yes to everything. In fact, I can't say yes to most ideas. Our organization would grind to a halt if we accepted even 5 percent of the proposals that come our way. Our ministry cannot lose its focus.

A church's ministry can lose its effectiveness if the leaders say yes to everything. The purpose of focus in the simple church is to say yes only to those areas that fall within the simple church process.

Focus is a truth taught and affirmed throughout Scripture. The focus of individuals in the Bible is humbling, and the principle of *one thing* emerges.

David prayed in Psalm 27:4, "I have asked one thing from the LORD; it is what I desire: to dwell in the house of the LORD all the days of my life, gazing on the beauty of the LORD and seeking Him in His temple." One thing was his focus. An intimate and passionate relationship with God consumed him.

Paul said in Philippians 3:13–14, "Brothers, I do not consider myself to have taken hold of it. But one thing I do: forgetting what is behind and reaching forward to what is ahead, I pursue as my goal the prize promised by God's heavenly call in Christ Jesus." One thing was his focus. The goal of Christlikeness compelled him to move forward in his spiritual journey. In fact, for Paul, everything else was filth compared to this one thing (see Phil. 3:8).

Paul likewise instructed Timothy to train himself to be godly. To do so, Timothy would have to avoid all the godless chatter and legalistic principles surrounding him. He had to focus on the one thing of being transformed by God (see 1 Tim. 4:7–8).

The writer of Hebrews instructs us to throw off sin and everything else that hinders us from running the race that Christ has marked out for us (see Heb. 12:1). One thing. The challenge is to get rid of anything that gets in the way of spiritual transformation.

Focus is thus the commitment to abandon everything else that falls outside of the simple ministry process. And here is where some leaders get confused and others get in trouble.

This fourth component of the simple church may involve some elimination of existing programs and ministries. Such eliminating can be difficult if not painful. It is easy for the author of the book

to talk about doing away with sacred cows. It's a lot more difficult for the leader of the church to eliminate someone's favorite
program or ministry. Such moves can engender pain, real pain. So
what's the answer?

First, be careful before adding something new to the list of
activities of the church. Saying no is easier than eliminating. And
sometimes the guilty party in adding to the church's full plate is
none other than the pastor or a staff member.

Second, focus does not mean that there has to be a mass elimination of programs and ministries. In Thom's church, Brentwood
Baptist Church in the Nashville area, there are a plethora of ministry and mission opportunities. But Brentwood, to some extent,
still practices the simple church model. The catch is that leaders
make clear that they do not expect the members to be involved
in all of these ministries. To the contrary, the leaders warn the
members not to try everything.

The members of Brentwood are urged to be involved in one
of the worship services, to connect with a Sunday school class or
small group, and to get involved in one ministry. Brentwood has
a lot going on, but it is still a simple church, especially through
the lens of those who attend.

Becoming Simple

This book is both descriptive and prescriptive. In the first
section of *Essential Church*, we looked at the malady of church
dropouts, focusing on the most likely dropouts, adolescents and
young adults. In this second section, we are offering prescriptions. Indeed, we believe that churches could see a much greater
evangelistic harvest and a much higher retention rate if they took
seriously the four key elements of the essential church: simplify,
deepen, expect, and multiply.

We want to emphasize that the structural issues of the church are not the most important. Indeed in some ways they are the least important of the four elements.

But structure is still important.

Do you remember Rachel at the beginning of this chapter? She lamented the confusion that seemed present in the churches she was visiting. Rachel was one of the dechurched we interviewed, and she was sincerely seeking to return to church.

But she is close to giving up.

Rachel will not get to doctrine and biblical teachings *(deepen)* because she can't get past the structure. Rachel will not hear what a true disciple of Christ looks like *(expect)* because she can't get past the structure. Rachel will not become an evangelistic and missional agent of God *(multiply)* because she can't get past the structure.

Get the picture?

That is why Thom and Eric advocated the simple church. They were not pushing a new program or a new fad or a new model. They were talking about having the right structure so everything else can fall into place. That is the essence of the simple church.

Is such change easy? In a word, no. Are such changes possible? In God's power, absolutely yes.

A recent medical study revealed just how difficult change is for people. Roughly six hundred thousand people have heart bypass surgery each year in America. These people are told after their bypasses that they must change their lifestyle. The heart bypass is a temporary fix. They must change their diet. They must quit smoking and drinking. They must exercise and reduce stress.

In essence, the doctors say, "Change or die."

You would think that a near-death experience would forever grab the attention of the patients. You would think they would vote for change. You would think the argument for change is so compelling that the patients would make the appropriate lifestyle alterations.

Sadly that is not the case. Ninety percent of the heart patients do not change. They remain the same, living the status quo. Study after study indicates that two years after heart surgery, the patients have not altered their behavior. Instead of making changes for life, they choose death.[2]

To Live or To Die

You read the dire statistics on the state of the American church earlier in this book. Simply stated, our churches are reaching fewer people and losing more people. We won't depress you further by repeating those numbers—except one:

> More than two-thirds of youth attending Protestant churches stop attending church between the ages of eighteen and twenty-two.

Our research is fallible, but that statistic is tough to refute. Our churches are dying. We have attempted through this project to look at the group we are losing the fastest and try to understand why we are losing them and what we can do to get them back.

At the risk of redundancy, we repeat that the structure is not the most important facet of a church. Doctrine is more important. Clear membership expectations are more important. Evangelism is more important. But each of those more important areas may not come alive in your church without the right structure.

If we ranked the most important parts of our physical bodies, the heart would be near the top. Or the brain. Or perhaps the lungs. But try to have a living human body without any bones, and you will see the importance of structure. The skeleton may not be the most important part of our body, but the more important parts cannot function without it.

The simple church is a well-researched and possible form of structure. We don't claim infallibility to this approach, but it is a structure that is working well in many churches.

Here is the challenge: structure tends to be the most difficult part to change in the church. But the decision could be one of life or death for the church.

Cluttered church leaders do not have the luxury to wait. And ceasing to be a pack rat will be extremely challenging. Moving out the clutter can be painful. Leadership expert Tom Peters once commented, "It is easier to kill an organization than it is to change it."[3]

Change is that difficult. The majority of heart patients choose not to change. They act as if they would rather die. In the same way the majority of churches choose not to change. They would rather die. Tragically, in most churches, the pain of change is greater than the pain of dying.

While moving to a healthy structure needs to happen, the transition will not be easy. It is change. In fact, it is the most visible change of the four elements of the essential church: simplify, deepen, expect, and multiply. Becoming a simple church is difficult. In fact, the longer your church has been complex, the more difficult the transition will be.

Please do not take the easy route. Don't look at our research on church dropouts as the rationale to make such rapid change that you kill the church in the process. You have seen that happen. It is horrible. Do not treat moving toward simple as a corporate restructuring or downsizing initiative. The church is the body of Christ, filled with real people with real feelings.

There is a tension here, isn't there?

On the one hand, you need to move to a simple structure as quickly as you can. So much depends on it. The longer you are complex, the longer your focus is divided. If you remain complex, your process for transformation remains unclear. The longer you are complex, the longer your church is congested. People remain unchanged. They do not move toward greater doctrinal depth. They do not understand the expectations of being a part of Christ's church. And they do not develop a passion to take the gospel to the nations and next door.

On the other hand, you must move to simple slowly. You have the heart of a shepherd, and you care for the people in your church. Becoming simple will be painful for some people. They cannot imagine losing some of the traditions and programs.

So the tension exists. You desire to see changes happen now for the sake of the kingdom and the unchanged people in your community. You want to see the dechurched become the rechurched. You desire to bring the people you already have along with you. How is this tension resolved?

Change theorists argue over this tension. Some advocate that change should happen all at once. Quickly. These people insist that it is less painful to cut off your arm with one fell swoop as opposed to one section at a time. They advise to tie all changes to an overarching vision and go for it. They believe that big sweeping changes produce results quickly, which ultimately validates the change.

Other change theorists shake their heads in disagreement to this advice. They believe change should be incremental, slow, and methodical. These people insist that the goal of change is not destruction but transformation. They believe that by implementing change slowly, people are given the opportunity to adapt and grow. They propose that incremental change is wise because each change builds a culture in which more change can occur.

Which group is right? Both approaches to change have succeeded. Both approaches to change have failed. You must live with this tension. Now/later. Fast/slow. Sweeping/incremental.

Good news. You have the Holy Spirit. Pray for discernment. Allow God to give you wisdom and grant you favor. Get on God's timetable. Move to a simple structure as God leads. Use wisdom and compassion in becoming a simple church so that your church may become an essential church.

But do something. It is a matter of life or death.

CHAPTER 8

Deepen: Getting the Content Right

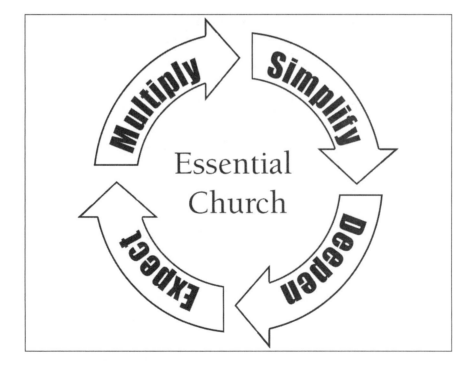

The call to vocational ministry in my (Thom's) life was rather dramatic. I was a twenty-seven-year-old, fifth-generation banker. I had risen rapidly in the banking world where, at that young age, I was vice president in charge of all of the corporate loans for the bank. If I could have scripted my life, I was playing the part perfectly.

We moved into our new home with one baby (Sam), and Art would be born shortly. Life was good.

But something was taking place that I did not fully understand. Something seemed to be pulling me in a different direction. At the time I didn't realize that Someone was pulling me in a different direction.

I tried to ignore the pull. My life was settling down. I was in church regularly. In fact, I had just been ordained as a deacon. I was on a decent spiritual path. It just didn't make sense that life should change.

Brian Clowers was a seven-year-old in a class that Nellie Jo and I taught at church. He had a heart defect that required open-heart surgery. I decided to visit him in the hospital after his surgery and to spend some time with his parents, Lynn and Elaine, who were our peers and friends.

I thought all was well. I didn't know that Brian would die as I got to his hospital room. I was not prepared for his parents to fall on my shoulders in anguish and grief.

But something else transpired at that moment.

What I had sensed and felt now became clear.

I was to minister to people like Lynn and Elaine the rest of my life. My vocational path had to change.

I was called to ministry.

When I arrived home from the hospital, still in shock and disbelief, Nellie Jo greeted me and hugged me. "Hey doll," I said softly. "Sit down. I need to talk with you."

Nellie Jo gave me that beautiful smile that attracted me to her the first time I saw her, and said, "God has called us into ministry, hasn't He?"

My mouth was probably wide open trying to speak, but Nellie Jo answered the unasked question.

"Of course I know. You don't think God would just speak to you about this matter, do you?"

We didn't wait around. We immediately put our house on the market. I gave my resignation to the bank, and they were gracious and allowed me to give three months' notice to get my life in order for the transition. After all, we needed to go to seminary.

Seminary? I had never set foot on a seminary campus. How would I know where to go? I began seeking advice.

Eventually I was confronted with two choices. I could go to a denominational seminary; Southern Baptists have six seminaries. Or I could go to a Bible seminary like Dallas Theological Seminary. A pastor who had been a great friend to me said, "It really depends on what type of church you want to be in. If you want to be in a denominational church where the focus is missions and evangelism, you should go with a Southern Baptist seminary. If you want to be in a Bible teaching church, you probably should look elsewhere."

That was the first time I had heard someone articulate that churches were specialists. Bible teaching or missions. Evangelism or discipleship. And as we articulated earlier, we see that dichotomy as false and harmful. The New Testament church must be both.

In chapter 10 we will discuss the multiplying church, the church that focuses on reaching neighbors and reaching the nations. But the purpose of this chapter is to talk about the teaching church, the church that leads its members deeper into biblical truths.

Hear us clearly. The church that will retain the younger generations does not have the luxury of choosing. The church must be a reaching and teaching church. It must multiply and deepen. It must be a New Testament church.

In the previous chapter we looked at the issue of structure, and we advocated the simple church, which is just another way of saying that we advocated a church that has a clear process of discipleship.

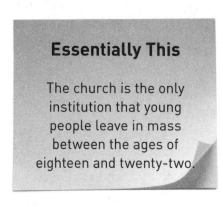

Essentially This

The church is the only institution that young people leave in mass between the ages of eighteen and twenty-two.

But when Thom and Eric Geiger wrote *Simple Church*, they said little about the *content* that must be taught in the process of discipleship. To use a human body analogy, the skeleton is important. It provides the necessary structure to support life. But the muscle and the organs and the circulatory systems are the life itself. Without them we would have nothing but dry bones.

Depth and Relevance Are Not Mutually Exclusive

I was told in the early 1980s that I needed to choose between a ministry of Bible teaching and a ministry of missions and evangelism. Today we are being told by some that we need to choose between a church that is relevant and one that teaches deep biblical truths.

Absurd.

Once again we are confronted with false dichotomies. Why can't a church be both relevant and deeply doctrinal? Why must we choose? Why *should* we choose?

If we try to replicate the church of the 1950s, we are unlikely to see a great inflow of young people. But if we don't offer them meaty, life-changing, biblical teaching, we won't keep them. They will be among the two out of three young adults between the ages of eighteen and twenty-two who "exodus" our churches.

The Anchor of God's Word Holds in Life's Transitions

One startling piece of our research told us volumes about why we lose so many young people at a critical juncture of their lives. Of those who left the church between the ages of eighteen and twenty-two, *97 percent left because of a life-change issue.* Read that percentage again: 97 percent left because of a life-change issue.

Most of the dropouts did not leave their families during this time.

Most of the dropouts did not leave their social networks during this time.

Most of the dropouts did not leave the educational system during this time.

But most of them did leave the church

Let's look again at some of the top life-change reasons that young people left the church. Remember, 97 percent of those who left indicated that the departure was due to one of nineteen life-change reasons. Here are the top ten.

Top Ten Life-Change Reasons Young Adults Left the Church between the Ages of Eighteen and Twenty-two

1. I simply wanted a break from church (27 percent).
2. I moved to college and stopped attending church (25 percent).
3. My work responsibilities prevented me from attending church (23 percent).
4. I moved too far away from the church to continue attending (22 percent).
5. I became too busy though I still wanted to attend (22 percent).
6. I chose to spend more time with friends outside the church (17 percent).

7. School responsibilities prevented me from attending
   (16 percent).

8. I wanted to make life decisions that were not accepted by
   the church (14 percent).

9. Family/home responsibilities prevented me from
   attending church (12 percent).

10. (tie) I lost touch with my churchgoing friends
    (11 percent).

10. (tie) Other activities/scheduling conflicts prevented me
    from attending church (11 percent).

Now let's hear from Max, and we will hear a stark contrast to the excuses of the dechurched in the top ten above. Max is now twenty-six years old. He is single but dating one woman "with serious intentions." Max is in the minority. He is among the three out of ten who did not drop out of church between the ages of eighteen and twenty-two.

"Yeah, I saw a lot of my friends drop out of different churches," Max began. "But I saw a majority of those at my church stay active in the church when the young adults at other churches were leaving in droves."

Max paused for a moment. He seemed uncomfortable with the direction of his conversation. "It sounds like I'm being condescending. You know, 'My church is better than the rest.' But I don't know how else to say it. At my church they get you into the Word, and you go deep into the Word. Frankly I saw a lot of good entertainment and good activities at the other churches. And that's fine. But if you're not anchored to the Word, you will drift away."

We asked Max to explain how the deep biblical teaching takes place at his church. He responded with enthusiasm.

"I came to the church when I was fourteen and my dad got a new job," he began. "The transition of uprooting my mom, my sister, and me was tough; but my parents helped a whole lot by working hard to find a good church. Boy did they succeed.

"When we first came to Grace Church, we had to go through a new members' class where they shared with us the expectations of members. They said we needed to be in a Sunday morning Bible study group and attend worship services. The leaders then told us that they offered several six-week small-group studies, and they encouraged their members to be in at least two of those a year. Finally, we were to be involved in one ministry, preferably through our Sunday morning Bible study group."

We could see the excitement in Max's eyes as he told us more about Grace Church.

"The purpose of the Sunday morning Bible study was clear. We were always studying a book of the Bible," he said. "In fact the church goes through the entire Bible in seven years. I have almost completed two cycles now."

"What about the small-group studies?"

"The church offers several small-group studies each year," Max responded. "Some of them deal with the doctrinal issues. Some with life application issues like marriage or money. And in some of them, you may study about other religions and cults, you know, apologetics stuff. But everything we study is biblically based."

We then gravitated to discussions about the preaching at Grace Church. "About two-thirds of Pastor Gills' sermons are expository messages that align with our Sunday morning Bible study," he said. And then Max's smile broadened. "That's when I really get it—when the sermon is based on the same passage we studied in Sunday school."

Are all of the pastor's sermons expository? "No," he told us. "Sometimes he preaches some great topical sermons, and on a few occasions he has preached a short series on a Christian doctrine. But most of the time he is preaching expositionally from the book we are studying on Sunday morning."

We were ready to ask Max some other questions, but he obviously was not done with this topic. "I think one of the greatest things Grace Church has done for me," he said with excitement, "is to encourage me to spend time in the Bible myself. They tell us again and again that the church should only be a supplement to a personal time of prayer and Bible study. That message really sticks."

We were finally ready to return to the original reason we began talking with Max. How has all of this "content" made a difference in his decision to remain active in the church? The answer was expected.

"The Word is so much a part of my life," Max said, "that studying it has become a life priority for me. And when I am dealing with tough decisions or life-changing situations, I can always remember something I have studied in Scripture to help me know how to deal with anything."

Max smiled. "And none of my studies in the Bible have ever told me to take a break from church. To the contrary, I realize that I need the church more than ever."

The Old Hypocrisy Issue

Most of the top ten reasons the dropouts left the church were related to life-change issues, but we cannot ignore one of the exceptions to that statement. In fact, it was the second most frequent response: "I left the church because the church members seemed judgmental or hypocritical." More than one-fourth (26 percent) of the dechurched offered the age-old hypocrisy response.

I (Thom) remember the first time I encountered such a response as a pastor. I cannot remember the woman's name, but I can still see the smirk on her face when I asked her to return to church: "Jesus and I are getting along just fine without all the hypocrites in that church."

Man, did that statement steam me! This woman was in her early forties and had not been in church for twenty years. (Not surprisingly, she was still on the membership rolls.) She was a church dropout, and she fit the pattern perfectly of those who typically drop out between the ages of eighteen and twenty-two.

I was tempted to tell her that she was the biggest hypocrite by forsaking church for so many years. I was tempted to repeat some of the rumors that I heard about her own lifestyle. (Can you still sense my emotions on an event that's more than twenty years old?) But I refrained—either from wisdom or desire for job security.

The point is that biblically grounded dropouts would know they are out of God's will. They could not neglect all of the apostle Paul's letters written primarily to local churches. They could not ignore the importance of the inception of the church at Jerusalem at Pentecost. And they could not deny the teachings of the writer of Hebrews in 10:24–25, just before he begins writing about willful disobedience: "And let us be concerned about one another in order to promote love and good works, not staying away from our meetings, as some habitually do, but encouraging each other, and all the more as you see the day drawing near."

Biblically grounded Christians recognize that all believers are hypocrites in the sense that we have not attained sinless perfection. And they thus recognize that they need the church even more. The excuse of hypocrisy can be a clear statement of one's own biblical illiteracy.

Other Indicators of Shallowness and Dropouts

While we would not suggest that all of the dechurched are biblically shallow, there is evidence that more of the dropouts fit that description than those who stayed in church.

Kenneth dropped out of church when he was nineteen. He is now a married man, twenty-five years old, with his first child on the way. "I have had some thoughts about returning to church," Kenneth told us, "especially with a kid on the way. I mean, I want to be a good example to him (we know it's a boy), but I'm still not sure that church is the best path for our family."

Kenneth continued, "I was in church every week until I turned nineteen. I didn't plan on leaving, but it just kind of happened, you know. Looking back, I can see that I didn't really agree with everything I heard. Like, one of my friends at the church insisted that the only way to God is to believe in Jesus. Where did they get that narrow-minded view?"

Perhaps Kenneth saw one of our raised eyebrows, but he didn't pause. "I have to be honest, guys. I can't tell you why I believed what I believed. I'm not even sure if I can call myself Christian. In fact, I even have doubts about the existence of God though I'm not ready to declare myself an atheist. I guess I am an agnostic."

Wow. We needed a few seconds to gather our composure.

Kenneth is well educated and articulate. He already has his MBA, and he is on a fast path in the corporate world. It was challenging for us to respond to him.

This dechurched, educated man could not articulate why Christians believe what they believe. He seemed unfamiliar with the basic claim of the exclusivity of salvation in Christ, such as those found in John 14:6 and Acts 4:12. He certainly could not tell us that he was a Christian even though he knew the meanings of atheism and agnosticism.

Kenneth was not grounded in the Scripture. I guess our biggest surprise was that he stayed in church as long as he did.

I (Thom) have done research that indicates that as many as one-half of church members may not be Christians, as least as they articulate their own beliefs.[1] We have little doubt that many of the young dropouts we have surveyed are not only weak in their grasp of biblical truths, but many of them, like Kenneth, may not be Christians at all.

Let's return to the survey of the dechurched and look at some of the other reasons they stopped attending church.

"I disagreed with the church's teachings about God"
(14 percent). We can assume that many of the

dechurched had the same reservations as those expressed by Kenneth. He couldn't see how Christians claim that Jesus is the only way to God.

"I was unsure of the reasons behind my faith" *(13 percent).* This statement is clear that one out of seven of the dechurched never understood the basics of the Christian faith.

"I no longer wanted to identify myself as a Christian" *(9 percent).* These respondents were not just ungrounded Christians; they were, by their own declaration, not Christians.

"I stopped believing in God" (7 percent). No further comments are necessary.

Back to the Main Man

We have made clear throughout this book the importance of the role of the pastor in stemming the tide of church dropouts. We are hesitant to keep mentioning this issue for fear that we may place an unnecessary burden on men who already have too many burdens and responsibilities.

Thom served as senior pastor of four churches. Sam serves the church as senior pastor as well. We both know the unrealistic expectations that are placed on pastors. Pastors are not only supposed to be omniscient; they are supposed to be omnipresent as well. Thom actually had a church member get mad at him because he was at another member's home who had just lost her husband. But the angry member insisted that Thom should have been at their class social function. Her telling comment? "You just need to figure out how to be more places at the same time!"

Omnipresence noted.

We can't escape the reality that God uses the pastor to cast a vision. He works through the pastor to set the tone in the church.

God uses the pastor as an example for others to follow. Sure, some churches won't follow good leaders no matter what. They would rather die than change. And they usually get the former for forsaking the latter.

Still, leadership matters. Leadership is critical. And the most visible aspect of leadership for the pastor takes place in the pulpit. For better or worse, the people in the church are watching and listening.

And most of them do not expect the pastor to have the oratory skills of a well-known pastor. They do not expect him to have the exegetical insights of some of the most brilliant preachers in the land.

But they do have expectations.

They expect pastors to be prepared in the pulpit. They know, for the most part, who's winging it and who has prepared. They expect the pastor to teach them about God's Word. In many ways the preaching event is sacred. The people want to hear from God and His Word. They expect the pastor to open the Bible and teach them what God says.

And they expect him to make the Bible relevant to their lives. While they may be fascinated by some esoteric doctrine, they ultimately want to know how God would have them apply His truths to their lives.

One of the most common complaints we hear about the beleaguered pastors from church members is, "I'm just not getting fed." Now we realize that some of those complaints are self-centered. We realize that some people will complain about everything and anything. And some people would find fault if the apostle Paul himself were preaching.

But the comment is telling.

"I'm just not getting fed." That means they are hungry. They are hungry for God's Word for their lives today.

That's what we are hearing from many of the dechurched. They were hungry, and they were not being fed. Sure, they could have and should have found a church where they could be fed, but we are dealing with the reality that they are dropouts.

One out of every seven dropouts said that the sermons did not capture their attention, and about the same number said that the church was not helping them to develop spiritually. Of the dropouts 8 percent stated bluntly that the pastor was not a good preacher and 7 percent said that the sermons were not relevant to their lives.

Taken individually, none of the responses was overwhelming; but taken in the aggregate, they are saying something powerfully. Preaching matters. The content of the sermons matters. And the life application of the sermons matters.

Any church or pastor who does not take seriously the role of preaching in his church is missing it. Just look at the dropouts as at least part of the evidence.

The Good News: Some Will Return

We have focused most of this book on the dechurched, those who have dropped out of church. But in the midst of all of our bad news, allow us to share some good news. Some of the dechurched will return to church.

We surveyed 617 young adults who had dropped out of church but eventually decided to return. The number one reason they gave for their return to church was encouragement from others. Four out of ten (39 percent) came back due to encouragement from parents or other family members. Another two out of ten (21 percent) returned because of encouragement from friends or acquaintances. When we eliminate the overlap of some responding to both reasons, we found that one-half (50 percent) returned because of encouragement from family or friends. We will look at this issue more fully in chapter 10.

But the second category of reasons for returning to church was fascinating. The rechurched simply told us that God convicted them to return to church. Here are the three responses related to this reason:

"I simply felt the desire to return" (34 percent).
"I felt that God was calling me to return to church"
    (28 percent).
"I felt convicted of the need to return to church"
    (16 percent).

Interestingly, women were more likely than men to offer these responses. In the first example above, 41 percent of the women cited the reason as compared to 22 percent of the men. In the second example, the response of females was 34 percent to 18 percent for males.

Ginger fits this description well. She dropped out of church when she was twenty, but she returned four years later. It is fascinating to hear her reasons for returning.

"I just sensed it was time for me to get back in church," Ginger began. "I have been married a year, but I haven't gotten my husband to attend with me. I miss the fellowship of Christians, and, frankly, I know I'm supposed to be in church. The Bible doesn't teach a Lone Ranger Christianity. I have really missed learning God's Word in Bible study groups and through the sermons."

Ginger continued, "I have decided that I will not nag my husband to attend. He is a good guy, but he can really be stubborn. I am praying that I can be the example of the godly wife in Scripture so that my walk with the Lord may influence him to return to church."

We are sure that you picked up some telling comments from Ginger. She knew that the Bible taught that she should be in church. She knew that the Bible said she should find fellowship with other Christians. And she knew that Scriptures taught what a godly wife should be.

Then Ginger told us that she missed Bible study and that she missed hearing God's Word preached. This rechurched lady obviously has some grounding in the Word of God. Though we don't know how she would fare on a Bible knowledge quiz, we do know that she has some level of understanding of Scriptures.

Deepen. Don't compromise on the teachings of Scripture. We do our young people (and all persons for that matter) a great disservice when we water down God's Word or, especially, fail to teach it at all.

Young people are more likely to come back to church if they have been grounded in Scripture. Similarly, young people are more likely *never* to leave church if they are taught the truths of God's Word. Let's review that group now.

The Better News: Some Young People Will Never Leave the Church

We have focused much attention on the two-thirds of young people who will leave the church between the ages of eighteen and twenty-two. That means one-third never drop out. What is the difference between the two groups? What prompts the latter group to remain involved in church?

Those who remain active in the church have two overarching reasons for staying: (1) they have a personal commitment to the church, and (2) they see the benefits of remaining in church. All of these relate to the biblical foundations they have.

For example, two-thirds (65 percent) of the churchgoers indicated that church was a part of their vital relationship with God. "That's where I am taught about God and His Word," Daniel related to us. "And it's where I connect with other Christians."

Well over half (58 percent) of this group said that the church provides them guidance for everyday decisions. "I can't imagine going any length of time," Denise said, "without hearing a sermon or being in a Bible study at church. I get my guidance from God and His Word."

More than four out of ten of the churchgoers (42 percent) told us that they remain at church because they are committed to the purpose and the work of the church. "The Bible teaches that we are to be a part of the body of Christ working together," A. J. said. "If I am not active in church, I am being deliberately disobedient."

A significant portion of the churchgoers saw the personal benefit of remaining at church. One half (50 percent) of them saw church as helping them become better persons, and one-fourth (24 percent) actually said that they were afraid to live a churchless life without the spiritual guidance it provides. "If I am faithful to the church and obey the teachings of God's Word," Karen remarked, "I simply am a better person. I am a better wife, a better mother, a better friend . . . just a better person all around."

The evidence is clear. The church and its teachings are a major reason people return to church. They are a major reason people never leave the church. And those who are not taught the depths and riches of God's Word are the most likely to enter the ranks of the dechurched.

The younger adults of today want deep biblical teachings. They want to hear the whole counsel of God. They want to hear truth, even if it makes them uneasy or uncomfortable.

In football "going deep" refers to a receiver running many yards in anticipation of catching the quarterback's long pass. The deep passes that are caught are the most spectacular and most likely to get the crowd on its feet. I (Thom) love to be at a football game with ninety thousand other screaming fans. I stand spontaneously when the long pass develops and when the wide receiver goes deep. And I scream at the top of my lungs if the pass is complete (but only if it's my team that's successful!).

Going deep is exciting in football.

Going deep is essential in church.

Let's review some important truths about going deep. In the last chapter of this book, we will offer some practical applications to make this step of the essential church a part of your congregation.

Summary 1. Depth and Relevance Are Not Mutually Exclusive

OK, we know we are a bit redundant on this point. But in our consultations and communications with churches across the nation, we hear the argument often. Many leaders think a church can't be "cool" and deep at the same time. Or some argue, just because the teaching is deep, it loses its relevance, that young people are turned off by such teaching and preaching.

As we have shown throughout this book, young people are more likely to drop out if the teaching is watered down. This generation is smart and eager to learn. They can and will learn the deep truth from Scripture. Let's not disappoint them.

Summary 2. One of the Healthiest Approaches to "Deep" Has Three Components

As we have worked with churches across the nation, we have observed those congregations that are highly intentional about communicating the depths of Scripture.

It still begins with the pastor.

Those pastors who excel at communicating God's Word spend much time in God's Word themselves. Unfortunately the demands of many church members pull pastors in so many directions that only the leftover time is given to Bible study and sermon preparation.

In Acts 6 the apostles were confronted with that reality even as the early church was just beginning. Do you remember the problem? "In those days, as the number of the disciples was multiplying, there arose a complaint by the Hellenistic Jews against the Hebraic Jews that their widows were being overlooked in the daily distribution" (Acts 6:1).

Simply stated, ministry was being overlooked. And the church was complaining, murmuring just like the Israelites in the wilderness. A group of widows who depended on the church for their meals was being overlooked. They likely expected the apostles to drop everything they were doing and take care of their needs. Pastors and church staff will undoubtedly recognize such an attitude!

But the apostles took another approach. They knew that if they became personally responsible for all the ministry needs, other areas of the church would suffer.

> *"Then the Twelve summoned the whole company of the disciples and said, 'It would not be right for us to give up preaching about God to wait on tables. Therefore, brothers, select from among you seven men of good reputation, full of the Spirit and wisdom, whom we can appoint to this duty. But we will devote ourselves to prayer and to the preaching ministry.'"* (Acts 6:2–4)

Instead of carrying the burden of meeting almost every ministry need themselves, the apostles selected twelve lay leaders to do the ministry. And note what the apostles spent their time doing: prayer and preaching. They recognized the importance of the preaching ministry, and they refused to neglect it.

But the church did not neglect the real ministry need. The widows could not starve. So the church unleashed the laity to do the work of ministry, and the apostles got back to the business of prayer and preaching.

And here is the good news. Not only did the widows get fed. Not only did the apostles get time to pray and preach. To top it off, the whole church was happy with the resolution: "The proposal pleased the whole company" (Acts 6:5). Imagine that. A church that is well fed with meals and God's Word is a happy church.

While "deep" preaching is normative in essential churches, it is likewise important for church members to be involved in small-group Bible studies. The healthy churches we have consulted and researched over the years all make small-group Bible study a priority. Some churches call it Sunday school; some call it small groups. Others use such nomenclature as connect groups, life groups, and home groups. The name is not the important issue. What is important is for churches to lead their members toward regular and ongoing Bible study.

The third component of essential churches that go "deep" is their encouragement and exhortation for all of their members to study the Bible on their own. Some churches, for example, suggest a weekly Bible reading for the members. Some lay out a plan where the members will read the Bible in a year. But the point is that the churches demonstrate that personal Bible study is critical in the spiritual maturity of believers.

So what have we discovered about Christians who hear good sermons each week, who are involved in small-group Bible study, and who study the Bible on their own? We have found that such Christians rarely drop out, that they rarely become part of the dechurched. And if they do, they are the most likely to return.

So how does an essential church establish an environment of deep biblical teaching? Such churches are churches of high expectations. And that is the subject of the next chapter.

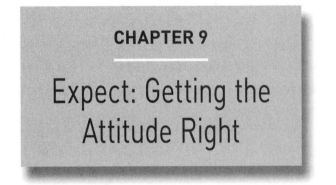

CHAPTER 9

Expect: Getting the Attitude Right

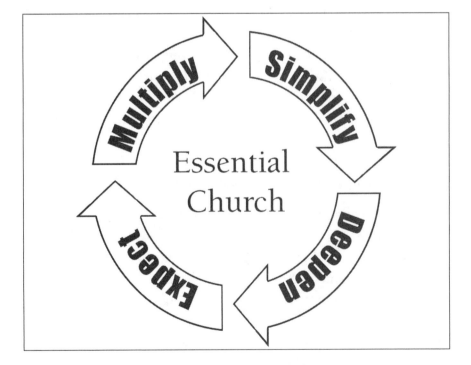

Karen and Jennifer are best friends. Their friendship began in the seventh grade and continued throughout high school and college. In fact, the two ladies chose a college where they could both pursue their different academic goals yet still stay together. They chose Union University in Jackson, Tennessee, and they both did well in their respective fields.

They are smart women. Finishing their course work in four years was easy for both of them, but graduation was difficult. They had five job offers between the two of them, but graduation meant they would have to be separated. None of the job offers were in the same cities.

"We knew this day would come," Karen lamented. "We are closer than most sisters, and we have cried together on many nights. But we knew that either jobs or husbands would probably put us in different locations. We were right," she sighed.

Jennifer is the more optimistic and upbeat of the two friends. "Hey, we have to be excited," she assured Karen. "We both have our dream jobs. We'll see each other often, I promise."

"Yeah, right," Karen deadpanned. "How much farther could we be apart and still be in the continental United States?"

Karen is moving to south Florida and Jennifer is moving to Washington state.

A Tale of Two Churches: Karen in Florida

Both of the ladies are Christians and, unlike the majority of the respondents in our study, they did not drop out of church when they graduated from high school. They were both active in the college ministry in a church in Jackson.

Though she misses Jennifer, Karen is happy with her move to south Florida. She loves the sunshine and the warmth. "I think I have SAD, you know, seasonal affective disorder," she told us. "The year-round sunshine is great. My whole attitude is different. I don't think I could ever leave this environment."

Karen began looking for a church soon after she moved to Florida. She found a Southern Baptist church that "felt comfortable" to her, and she joined the church after visiting a few weeks. She is a lifelong Southern Baptist so "it just seemed like the right thing to do."

We asked her what was involved in joining the church. "Oh, I just came forward during the invitation time and filled out a card. The church members came to the front to shake my hand and welcome me to the church."

And then what?

"Nothing else," she smiled.

No new members' class? No small-group connection? No ministry involvement process? No follow up?

"No, nothing else."

Karen dropped out of the church after seven months and has not returned to any church. "I really don't feel that guilty," were her words, but her face betrayed her conversation. "There is so much to do on Sunday in South Florida, and I still pray and read my Bible."

A Tale of Two Churches: Jennifer in Washington

Jennifer has an adventurous spirit. She had never traveled to the Northwest until she interviewed for her job in Washington. She loved moving to a new area and new culture even though she has deep West Tennessee roots. "They make fun of my Southern drawl," she laughed. "But that's OK because it's all done in good spirits."

We asked Jennifer how she likes the Northwest. "I absolutely love it," she exclaimed. "It's different from anything I have ever experienced, but it's a great place to be. I can see myself living here for ten years or more."

After hearing about Karen's church experience, or nonexperience now, we were expecting the worst from Jennifer. We were surprised.

"I am involved in the most wonderful church," she told us with obvious enthusiasm. "I couldn't find a Southern Baptist church so I ended up in a nondenominational church that has mostly Baptist beliefs."

We asked her if she is active in the church. "Wow. I am more active than I have ever been," Jennifer responded. "When I left the Bible Belt, I was really in need of the fellowship of other Christians. It took me a while to find the church, but it was love at first sight. I have never been in a place with more dedicated believers."

We then asked her about the process of becoming a member of her church. She anticipated our next question with her response. "It's a high-expectation church," Jennifer said. "You apply for membership and then attend a four-hour membership class on either four consecutive Sunday mornings or one Saturday morning."

She continued so we did not have to ask the obvious question. "They packed a lot in the four hours," she began. "They tell you about the mission of the church. They speak about thirty minutes on the history of the church and connected it to the mission. They talked about their small-group structure and how we are expected to be a part of it. And they really emphasized their outreach in the community and in the world."

Jennifer paused for a moment, but her excitement did not abate. "I have never been to a church where they make so clear what is expected of you and why it is expected. They spent the entire last hour telling us what membership at our church looks like."

At this point in our research, we could almost anticipate what Jennifer would tell us next. We would have been close in our prediction.

The mission statement is critical in the life of the church because it explains the discipleship process: "Worship the one true God, connect with other believers, grow deeper, and reach out to the world." They tell the new members to remember four key words: *worship, connect, grow,* and *reach*. But the church leaders emphasize "one true God" since *god* means so many different things to different people in the community.

The church expects members to be involved in an open Bible study group on Sunday morning. By its definition the group is ongoing and open to new participants at any point. About one-half of the groups meet on campus; but, due to lack of space, the others meet nearby in homes and restaurants.

The church expects the members to be involved in at least two discipleship groups a year. Most of the discipleship groups take place in off-campus locations and are typically six weeks in duration. The discipleship topics range from doctrinal teachings to current apologetic issues.

The church expects the members to attend a worship service each week. Currently the church has three worship services on Sunday morning, and they are looking to expand to a fourth service on Sunday night.

The church expects the members to be involved in at least one outreach or mission effort each year. The church has a variety of ongoing community outreach and international mission efforts.

Jennifer finds the expectations reasonable but necessary. "Some churches are so nonchalant about membership that they don't know where two-thirds of their members are," she noted with expertise. "And some are almost legalistic with their requirements. I think my church has found the right balance. I am expected to be in a Bible study and worship service on Sunday morning. I am expected to be in at least two six-week discipleship groups a year. And I am expected to be involved in at least one mission trip or community outreach effort. I can do more of course, but the minimum expectations are really not that bad."

Jennifer also appreciated the concise but thorough approach of the new members' class. "Our class was called 'Entry' and it was great," she told us. "The church could have made the entry longer and more difficult, but they were able to establish membership expectations in just a few hours."

The Essential Church: Expectations Clarified

Let's return to some of the reasons the dechurched left the church during the critical ages of eighteen to twenty-two. The number one reason, cited in different ways, is that the young adult simply did not see that church was essential to his or her life.

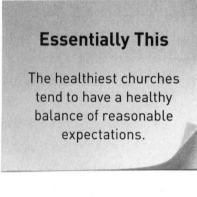

Essentially This

The healthiest churches tend to have a healthy balance of reasonable expectations.

"I simply wanted a break from church" (27 percent).

"I moved to college and stopped attending church" (25 percent).

"Work responsibilities prevented me from attending church" (23 percent).

"I moved too far from the church to continue attending" (22 percent).

"I became too busy even though I still wanted to attend" (22 percent).

"I chose to spend more time with friends outside the church" (17 percent).

"School responsibilities prevented me from attending church" (16 percent).

The pattern is obvious. The dechurched no longer saw church as a priority in their lives. Every "reason" is also an excuse. Imagine substituting the word *job* for *church* in each of the examples above. We doubt that someone could keep their job for any length of time offering such explanations.

So what is the solution? How does the church move toward higher expectations? How does the attitude change in a church that has expected little of its members? Obviously, one's place of vocation has the power of the paycheck. If you choose not to show up to work, the company can choose to stop paying you. That is not an option with the local church, but the congregation can change its "attitude."

Most of recent American church history has been one of the low-expectation churches. Because the local church was comprised mostly of volunteers, leaders have been reticent to create an environment and attitude of expectations. As a consequence, membership expectations have been communicated with extreme caution, if at all, lest the members become offended and leave.

This low-expectation environment has been normative for most of the churches in which young adults have attended. Most of them have heard little, if any, of what is expected of them as a church member. As a consequence they have seen church as a low priority or even optional.

Becoming a higher expectation church is vital in becoming an essential church. We learned this reality from the young adults who did not leave the church.

Toward the Higher-Expectation Church: Learning from Churched Young Adults

Our research included a survey of 406 young adults who stayed in church during the critical ages of eighteen to twenty-two, and who have remained in church since then. What are some of the primary reasons these young adults stayed in the church?

Church is a vital part of my relationship with God (65 percent). Two-thirds of the respondents could not see themselves as vibrant Christians without being an active part of a local congregation. They eschewed the attitude of the Lone Ranger Christian and embraced the biblical model of the local-church Christian. They understood that no local congregation is perfect; but they, nevertheless, chose to be imperfect Christians participating in an imperfect church.

This large majority of churched young adults viewed the church as crucial to their relationship with God. They simply did not compartmentalize the church as a different activity apart from a meaningful relationship with God; they saw church as essential to that relationship.

I wanted the church to help guide my decisions in everyday life (58 percent). A significant majority of the churched young adults indicated that the church was essential in the ongoing decisions of life.

"I can't imagine not having a church body to help me in life," noted twenty-eight-year-old Jack Witham. "Sometimes I simply need other Christians in the church to pray for me in an important decision. On other occasions my small-group Bible study has been a time where the Word has guided me in something. And almost every week I hear from God during our worship services. Plain and simple: church is essential to my life."

There it is again. *Church is essential to my life.* Church is not optional. Church is not auxiliary. Church is not peripheral. No, church is essential. It is a major part of the believer's life. And the Christian cannot imagine life without the support of a local congregation.

I felt that church was helping me become a better person (50 percent). One-half of the churched young adults pointed to clear evidence that the local congregation was developing them spiritually into becoming better persons. The essential nature of the church is evident again. We go to places where we can become healthier, happier, and better. And church was viewed as one of those places necessary for personal improvement.

I was committed to the purpose and work of the church (42 percent). Later in this chapter we will examine the relationship between a clear church purpose and retention of members.

The obvious reality is that church members must know their church's purpose before they can become committed to it. Unfortunately, in most American churches, the understood purpose of the church is vague if recollected at all. These churched young adults told us that they not only knew the purpose of the church; they embraced that purpose as well.

Church activities are a big part of my life (35 percent). We would expect that, for those who viewed the church as essential to their lives, they would also note that church activities were a major part of their lives. Such was the case with more than one-third of the churched young adults.

The role of church activities in different generations of churchgoers is fascinating. For the builder generation, those born before 1946, one was active in church to demonstrate loyalty to the church. Activity was thus tantamount to obedience. But for young adults today, church activity is the consequence of obedience. If the church is essential to one's life, if the church has a clearly understood purpose, and if the church is truly missional in all that it does, then the young adult will more likely be active. But that same young adult would rarely consider activity an act of obedience. Activity is the consequence of the church's being a meaningful part of one's life.

The church helped me through a difficult time in my life (30 percent). The essential church is truly the body of Christ. And during difficult times in one's life, many members of the body are there to help. Even at the young age of the twenty-somethings, nearly one-third had experienced a difficult time. And the church was there for them. And that is one of the reasons they are still with the church today.

I was afraid of living a life without spiritual guidance (24 percent). It would seem that one-fourth of the churched young adults get it, if not more. They see church as so essential to their lives that they cannot imagine getting spiritual guidance without the local congregation. In a day when fewer believers are viewing the local church as important, a significant minority of young adults think otherwise.

We must keep in mind that most of these young adults are in churches that *are* making a difference in lives and in the community. These are not churches that are simply going through the motions. These are not the churches that have meaningless meetings. These are not the churches that have little expectations of their members.

No, these are essential churches. And essential churches are, by their nature, higher-expectation churches. Of course the obvious question arises: What does a higher-expectation church look like? On the one hand such a question defies a simple answer. The higher-expectation church has some intangibles that are difficult to see. After all, what does an environment of expectation really look like?

On the other hand, certain manifestations of higher expectation are common in many essential churches. But a word of caution is in order. As we describe some of the things a higher-expectation church may do, please do not see these manifestations as a cookie-cutter mold for your church. Most of these essential churches worked prayerfully and tirelessly to get where they are today. And many had to discard approaches that just did not work at their churches. To repeat a cliché, one size does not fit all.

With that note of caution, it is instructive to see some of the approaches to higher expectations of the essential church. To that we now turn.

Essential Churches and Expectations

We have both learned, after a combination of nearly three decades of research, that merely presenting the facts and the numbers leaves unanswered questions. In fact, the most frequently asked question Thom received after coauthoring *Simple Church* was: Can you tell me some churches that are doing this so I can see what they are doing? Plain and simple, they want to know what a church looks like that matches our research. They hope that, in discovering the methodologies of other churches, they can apply some of the same methodologies to their churches.

And now that we have given the warning against becoming a cookie-cutter church, we can present some of the major methodologies of high-expectation essential churches. This overview is not sufficiently exhaustive, but it does provide insights into some of the most frequently used approaches.

The Vital Importance of the Actionable Mission Statement

Nearly a decade ago, Thom did research on churches that had high-expectation environments.[1] These churches were effectively evangelistic and had above-average retention rates. One of the cogent findings of the study was that the churches had a clearly understood mission or purpose statement. More than 64 percent of the churches had these mission statements that were not only written but understood and embraced by the congregation as well.[2]

After ten years we can say that the trend continues in healthy churches. But the point is that the mission statement leads to action. That is one of the significant findings in the research of *Simple Church* we just discussed.[3] A mission statement alone is of little value unless it can be clearly understood by the congregation and unless it leads to specific action.

Let's return to the example of Jennifer earlier in the chapter. Jennifer became an active and enthusiastic member of a nondenominational church in Washington state. When we asked her questions about the church, she quickly told us about the mission statement. Jennifer had been at the church less than six months, yet she knew the mission statement by heart.

"What is the mission statement of your church, Jennifer?"

She quickly responded, "'Worship the one true God, connect with other believers, grow deeper, and reach out to the world.'

They tell new members to remember four key words: *worship, connect, grow,* and *reach*." How can such a new member remember with precision the statement? Jennifer and others in the church remember because the statement is also their discipleship process.

"Worship the one true God." Members are expected to attend worship services each week.

"Connect with other believers." Members attend an open Bible study on Sunday mornings.

"Grow deeper." Those in the church are a part of a D-group (discipleship group) at least twice a year. Most D-groups are six weeks in length.

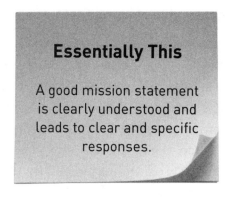

Essentially This

A good mission statement is clearly understood and leads to clear and specific responses.

"Reach out to the world." Members go on at least one international mission trip a year, or they are involved in some type of community outreach or ministry.

Mission statements have been around in churches for decades. Some are nicely printed in a beautiful frame on the wall, but no one knows a thing about them. Others were formed by task forces that spent weeks devising just the right verbiage. The church then voted on the statement with enthusiasm, but nothing happened beyond that.

Some mission statements mean something. They are actionable. These statements are found in essential churches where the dropout rate is low.

Leading Members to Small Groups

One of the most common and clearest signs of a higher-expectation church is the encouragement of members to move into small groups. When Thom did his study on high-expectation churches, he found that the small group was the highest correlative factor in member retention.[4] In that particular study he focused on the small group that was called the Sunday school in most of the churches. Since then we have found that the same principle applies in all open Bible study groups whether they are called Sunday school or some other name.

The small group connects people relationally, something that is difficult to achieve in a larger worship service. Many small groups function as smaller churches within the church. They may be the primary ministry arm to those in the group. They may have their own outreach ministry beyond their own group. They may have prayer groups.

The point is that the expectation of a person being in a small group is vital toward retention of those in the church. Once they build relationships in that small group, the likelihood of their departure drops significantly.

In Thom's earlier study on high expectations, his research team reviewed the records of hundreds of church members who had become Christians five years earlier. We then asked the staff if the persons were primarily attendees in worship services only or if they were in small groups as well. (In this study the small group was the Sunday school.) The contrast between the two groups was stark and amazing.

Those who were in a small group and attended worship service were *five times* more likely to be active in church than those who attended worship services alone.[5]

More than eight out of ten of the members who were active in a small group were still in the church five years later. But only two of ten were still active in the church five years later if they attended worship services only. (The numbers were adjusted for deceased members and those who moved out of the community.)

The graph below shows the dramatic difference between the two groups. The conclusion is basic and simple. If a member does not become involved in a small group, he or she is likely to become one of the dechurched.

The Growth of New Members' Classes in Essential Churches

Where do expectations begin in an essential church? Certainly the church leaders play a major role in the information they communicate and the manner in which they communicate expectations. But the formal beginning of expectations takes place in a new members' class. We realize that these classes have a number of names: Beginnings, 101, Vision Class, Inquirers' Class, Purpose Class, to name a few. For simplicity we will refer to them as either a new members' class or an entry class.

These classes are not always for new members or prospective members. Some churches make them available for those who simply have an interest in the church. But the purpose of the class is essentially the same from church to church. Those who attend are introduced to two aspects: information and expectations.

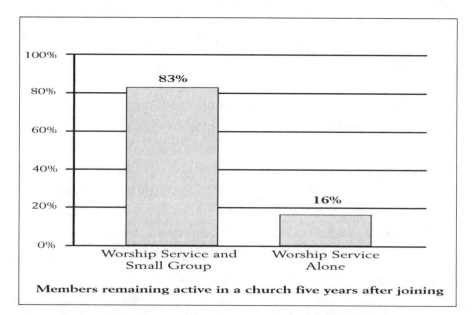

Members remaining active in a church five years after joining

The informational aspect of the class may include a history of the church, the beliefs of the church, and the ministries of the church, to name a few. The expectation part of the class lets those present know how they can become members of the church and what is expected of members. That latter aspect is critical in the essential church. Many of the dechurched today tell us that they never heard what was expected of them. They thus "fell through the cracks" without anyone noticing.

Church membership rolls are filled with unknown names, people who moved a decade ago, and even the deceased. In my own denomination, we estimate that as many as five million of our sixteen million members cannot be located.

I (Thom) learned this reality in my first church. I served as the pastor of a small, rural church in southern Indiana. We had about 150 members on the roll, but our average attendance at the time was less than twenty. I asked five of the long-term members of the church to review the names on the roll. We were only able to identify ninety of the members. Of those ninety members, about fifty still lived in the community but were considered "inactive members" (whatever that means).

I shared my plight with a local Methodist pastor who decided to conduct the same exercise in his church. When he and some long-term members reviewed the roll, they discovered about seventy of the infamous inactive members. Over coffee at a small restaurant, the Methodist pastor and I devised a plan. We would share each church's inactive list so the list could become a prospect list for the other church. We reasoned that it would be almost impossible to get our own inactive members back so we would let the other church treat them as prospects!

When we exchanged the lists, we looked at the names. Much to our surprise, we found sixteen people who were on both inactive lists. These people had managed to join a Methodist church and a Baptist church and then become inactive in both of them with no one noticing!

I volunteered to call the sixteen double inactive members to see if I could persuade them to go to either of their churches. In the process, I discovered that five of them were now Presbyterians. They had membership in three churches!

The point of my less-than-humorous story is to demonstrate how meaningless membership is in many churches. The good news is that entry classes are reducing the number of dechurched by establishing expectations early in the membership process. The most effective membership classes are brief, four or five hours, but they are sufficient to communicate both information and expectations.

In my previous study on high expectations, we examined the content of membership classes. Though the following information came from the earlier study, it is consistent with what we are seeing in churches today.[6] The major exception is item 16: explanation of the church's mission statement. We see that information included in virtually all essential churches today.

Topics Included in the New Members' Class

1. Doctrine/beliefs of the church (67 percent)
2. Polity/government of the church (66 percent)
3. Church constitution and bylaws (65 percent)
4. Purpose of the Lord's Supper/Communion and baptism (64 percent)
5. Church covenant and church discipline (63 percent)
6. Expectations of members (59 percent)
7. History of the church (57 percent)
8. Tour of church facilities (56 percent)
9. Denominational information (if applicable) (52 percent)
10. How to become a Christian (49 percent)
11. Budget/financial support of church (47 percent)
12. Requirements for church membership (39 percent)
13. Ministry opportunities in the church (37 percent)

14. Overview of spiritual disciplines (35 percent)
15. Introduction to church staff (34 percent)
16. Church's mission statement (33 percent)
17. Spiritual gifts inventory (30 percent)
18. Support of missions (21 percent)
19. Brief evangelism training (19 percent)

As prospective members attend these classes, they not only discover factual information about the church, but they also learn the personality of the church, and they learn what is expected of them. Those higher expectations lead to more young adults staying with the church.

The Essence of Expectation: Making a Difference

I (Thom) have watched the generational transition from two perspectives. I observed my parents' faithful church attendance. For the most part they were at church when the doors were open. They didn't, to my knowledge, question why the church did what it did. They just showed up. They were intensely loyal to the institution.

As a baby boomer born in 1955, I have some of that same institutional loyalty as my parents. When Sam, Art, and Jess were born, Nellie Jo and I had the three boys at church when the doors were opened. I was a businessman before I became a vocational minister, and I typically responded positively to the requests of the pastor and staff. But my loyalty was not blind. I began to wonder why my church did some of the things it did.

For example, I began to dread Sunday evening worship. My wife and I would work to the point of frustration to get the preschool boys ready for church on Sunday morning. When we came home from the services, we were ready to eat and crash. But at 5:00 p.m., we would have to get the boys ready again for another worship service at 6:00 p.m.

I summoned the courage to ask my pastor one day why we had Sunday evening services. Though I did not tell him, I could discern that he put little effort into that second message of the day. It may have been reruns of sermons from a previous church. The music was not strong either. It seemed like we had people singing in the evening service that we would never hear in the morning service.

In my naïveté I asked my pastor why we had that evening service. I don't remember his response, but I know it did not make sense to me. I remember the look on his face. It was as if failure to attend the Sunday evening service was the eighth mortal sin. How dare I question what the church has always done!

My parents would not have asked the question. I asked the question but continued to attend. My boys would not have attended as adults unless they saw a clear and meaningful purpose to what they were doing.

Such has been the generational transition. And that reason, more than any other, may explain the increased rate of young adult dropouts in the church. They simply don't think the church matters anymore. It is not essential.

Many, perhaps most, churches in America are irrelevant to the young people of today. They don't understand why churches do what they do. And if the church does not offer a plausible explanation, they leave. They will simply not waste their time in a church that is going through the motions. Institutional loyalty is dead.

What are the young adults looking for in a church today? They are looking for a church that is making a difference in the lives of its members. They are looking for a church that is making a difference in the community and around the world. And they are looking for a church where they can make a difference.

That is the difference in the lives of Karen and Jennifer you met at the beginning of this chapter. Karen joined a church where the only requirement was to complete a membership card, and someone did that for her. No one ever encouraged her to join a small group. No one ever asked her to get involved in a ministry. She never really learned what the church was all about.

So she left. She did not leave for another church. She just left. And now Karen is practicing her solo Christianity with little guilt; at least that's what she tells us. A lifelong church member, Karen joined the ranks of the dechurched after more than twenty-five years of being in a church.

Jennifer is in a new culture out of her comfort zone, but she has found a church that is impacting the lives of its members and the community in which it is located. It is a church that expects its members to make a difference.

Jennifer learned early in her experience at the church that she should get involved in a small group. She quickly developed close relationships that became part of the glue that has caused her to stick with the church. She is growing as a Christian in her small groups and in the five D-groups she has attended thus far. And she is developing a love for her community through one of the outreach ministries she recently joined. We have little doubt that, if she still lives in the area, we will find Jennifer active and happy in her church.

"You know," Jennifer told us, "everyone wants to make a difference. I don't know anyone who wants to go through life without having some impact. If most churches would just get that reality. If they would lead their members to make a difference, I believe that churches across America would be bursting at the seams with people who want to be there. People just want to make a difference."

The Essential Church, Continued

We have reviewed the dismal reality of church dropouts in America. And we have seen that the ranks of the dechurched are growing. Church is just not essential to many young adults today.

We have seen the hope that some churches offer. These churches have structures that make sense, structures that members can understand and embrace. We called this facet of the essential church "simplify."

We then looked at the reality that content does not matter. The teaching and preaching of the church are critical. Essential churches thus seek to "deepen."

And then in this chapter, we looked at the attitude of essential churches. These churches believe they can make a difference, and they believe their members can make a difference. This part of the essential church cycle is called "expect."

We now complete the cycle by looking at a critical aspect of essential churches. They are not stagnant. They don't just care for their own. They are not inwardly focused. But we are getting ahead of ourselves. Please join us in the next chapter as we celebrate the reality that essential churches "multiply."

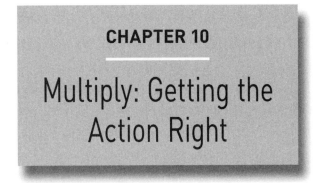

CHAPTER 10

Multiply: Getting the Action Right

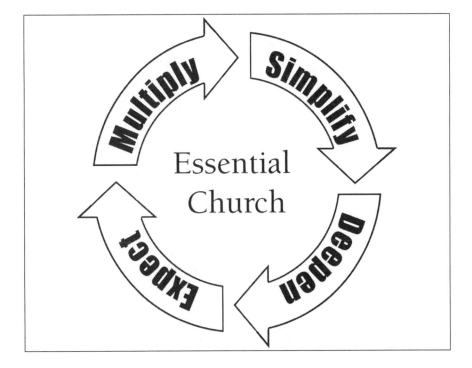

Evangelism. Say the word in a crowd and the reactions will be mixed, but most people will have a reaction. Some will respond with excitement: "That's the Great Commission. That's what all Christians and churches should be doing!" Others may respond with a stereotype of evangelistic Christians: "Yeah, I've seen those types. They try to grab you on the streets and cram some stuff down you."

Still others view evangelism as a narrow-minded theological reality. They see Christians as offensive, and they see an exclusive gospel as the most offensive. Our team recently conducted interviews with hundreds of lost and unchurched persons in North America. The response of Becky from Ontario, Canada, typifies this attitude: "Aren't Christians supposed to be nice? My impression is that Christians are snotty. Also, my first impression of preachers is that they are scary. Christians just think they are better than anyone else."[1]

Regardless of perspectives, two realities are clear. First, evangelism is not an option for Christians or for churches. The Great Commission is a mandate. Second, every church we have studied that is effectively reaching and retaining young adults is highly intentional about evangelism. No exceptions. Period.

Of course, methods of evangelism vary. We did not see a cookie-cutter approach in any of the churches we have studied. But we did see a passion for reaching people who are without Christ. We did witness churches that make evangelism a high priority in their ministries.

Essential churches have simple structures that can be understood and embraced. Essential churches strive to take their members into deeper biblical truths. Essential churches have an environment of high expectations of members. And essential churches seek to multiply, to reach beyond their own fellowship.

Reclamation as Multiplication

You have read the bad news in this book. We are losing young adults in our churches at an alarming rate. There is no need to repeat the dismal statistics here, but now we have some good news. Those who left are some of the most likely to return. We surveyed those who dropped out at ages eighteen to twenty-two when they reached the ages of twenty-three to thirty. And we found a definitive pilgrimage back to church.

Nearly two-thirds of the dechurched had become rechurched; at least they were rechurched in the sense that they were attending church a minimum of once a month by the time they reached the ages of twenty-three to thirty.

Simply stated, one of the most receptive fields toward multiplication in a church is the young adult group who dropped out a few years earlier. Most churches do little to reach this group. But a few churches are effective. They are the essential churches. Let's look at some of their approaches.

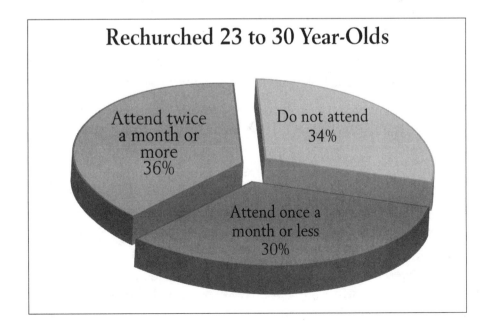

Rechurched 23 to 30 Year-Olds

- Attend twice a month or more 36%
- Do not attend 34%
- Attend once a month or less 30%

The Key to Reclamation: Friends and Family

We interviewed 394 rechurched young adults to find out why they returned to church. One myth that could be easily dismissed is that they were too angry at the church to return. To the contrary, the rechurched told us in overwhelming numbers that anger at the church was not a factor in their departures. Apathy always tended to be the trump card over anger.

So the dechurched often just needed a gentle nod to become the rechurched. And that gentle nod came most often from friends and family. Nearly four out of ten (39 percent) rechurched told us that parents or other family members were instrumental in their return to church. Another two out of ten (21 percent) said that they returned to church after friends or acquaintances encouraged them to attend.

If we eliminate the overlapping responses, *we find that exactly one-half (50 percent) of the rechurched are back in church because of the encouragement of a friend or family members*. It is easy to pass by the previous sentence with little reaction, but it is a profound reality. We lose two-thirds of our young adults between the ages of eighteen and twenty-two, but we can reclaim half of them with simple encouragement from family and friends.

Can the churches play a role in this encouragement to return? Indeed, we found that churches *must* play a role. Here are some helpful insights we learned from essential churches that have successfully reclaimed numbers of young adults:

Churches must have the right context for these returning young adults. "This is not your father's church in terms of worship style and approaches to ministry," one essential church pastor told us. "We are not compromising the Word, but we are making the changes to reach this age group. Our worship style has changed, and we have a Tuesday night worship service that is specifically geared as a place of reentry into the church." Simply stated, encouragement from friends and family for the young adults to return will be of little value if the church is mired in a time warp in the 1960s or 1970s.

Many churches recognize the social nature of these young adults and adjust accordingly. They are the Starbucks generation. They gather and chat at places that are often called third places. We noted earlier that the first place of social activity is the home, and the second place is where the young adults work. But they are drawn to a third place like Starbucks. And many leaders are recognizing that a third place can easily take place in the church. "A coworker invited me to have coffee

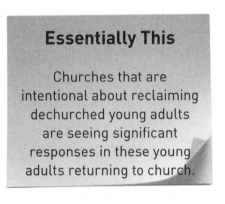

Essentially This

Churches that are intentional about reclaiming dechurched young adults are seeing significant responses in these young adults returning to church.

with him at The Gathering, a coffee shop in the church," Mike told us. "That really helped me ease back into the church. It just seemed natural to start attending his church after I had been in The Gathering a few times."

Some churches are pleasantly persistent in their reminders for members to invite friends and family to church. "Almost every month Pastor David reminds us to invite someone we know to church," Joanne shared with us. "It's a part of the DNA of the church."

We encountered a few churches that have focused prayer times for God's Spirit to work in the lives of friends and family who are being invited to return to church. The power of prayer is evident in many of these churches. "It is absolutely amazing," Donna exclaimed. "We will pray for these people by name, and then we see them show up at church a few weeks later. That excites us to pray even more."

The Power of the Invitation

Before we move too far from this topic of inviting dechurched young adults to return to church, let's look for a few minutes at the power of simply inviting people to church. In an earlier research project, our team interviewed more than three hundred unchurched persons across North America. One of the questions we asked them was simply, "If a Christian friend or family member invited you to a church function now, how likely would you be to attend?"[2] Look at these amazing responses:

Very Likely	31%
Somewhat Likely	51%
Not Likely at All	18%

These respondents included primarily the *never churched*, not the dechurched we have examined in this book. Eight out of ten (82 percent) indicated that they were at least somewhat likely to attend church if invited. And nearly one-third (31 percent) said they were very likely to attend if invited.

We realize that what people say they might do and what they will actually do may not be the same. But what if the numbers above are accurate by only half? That would still mean that four out of ten unchurched will attend church if invited. And we have anecdotal evidence that indicates the number is actually higher.

In follow-up research we discovered one additional element that can increase the response of a dechurched or unchurched person coming to church. They are much more comfortable if the person who invites them walks into the church facilities with them the first time they attend.

If we invite them, they will come. That one factor may be the most significant key in getting the dechurched young adults to return.

Life Events Are Key Opportunities to Get the Young Adults to Return

Our research confirmed the work of several previous projects plus the conventional wisdom of many: people are more receptive to make changes in their lives when they experience a significant life event.

Thomas was twenty-four years old when he made the decision to return to church. He married his high school sweetheart two years earlier, and now she was pregnant with their first child. Thomas never really got mad at the church. When he went to college, he just stopped attending. His wife had gently encouraged him to return to church after they married, but the announcement of her pregnancy was the deciding factor.

Both Thomas and his wife returned to church shortly before the child was born. They have been active in church ever since.

The year was 1979. And I (Thom) was that young man. The child that would be born on February 23, 1980, is the coauthor of this book.

Some of our research is basic conventional wisdom. We have known it for years, and the rechurched young adults confirmed it for us. Life events are key times when people start attending church or when they decide to return to church.

Let's return to our interview sample of 394 rechurched young adults. Look at the reasons they decided to return:

"I had children and felt it was time for them to start attending" (24 percent).

"I got married and wanted to attend with my spouse" (20 percent).

"I had a crisis in my life (death in the family, etc.)" (11 percent).

We easily grasp the reality that people are more likely to return to church during key life events. We nod with affirmation when we read such statistics as those above for the young adults.

But what do we do about it in our churches? What actions can we take?

One church in Florida noticed that the demographics of its community were getting younger. Younger families were purchasing the older homes of senior adults who were either moving to more affordable locations or who had passed on. The first trickle of these young families was noticeable in the older, more established churches.

When one of the young families visited, some of the members noticed that the young lady was pregnant, with birth obviously imminent. Some of the members asked her if they could deliver meals to the family after the baby was born. Surprised at the gesture, the young mother eagerly accepted. She had no family within twelve hours of her home.

When the mother returned from the hospital, three church members were waiting to deliver several precooked meals for the family of four. They continued that pattern for a few days. Having won her trust, one of the church members asked if she could watch the three-year-old daughter to give the mother a break from looking after the baby and the three-year-old. That pattern continued for several days.

After that a church member would call once or twice a week to see what needs the young mother had. In about six weeks the entire family showed up at church. They have been there ever since.

The young mother is now a leader in the church in a ministry that is having an impact in the community. It is called BAM (Baby Alert Ministry), and it is specifically geared to minister to new mothers during the first six weeks after the birth of a child.

The church was sorely lacking in young families until this ministry began. But now the demographics of the church are getting younger. And the church is taking small but significant steps to adjust its worship services and its other ministries to reach and keep this younger population.

That is but one example among many where churches are specifically targeting young adults during major life events. Sadly, few churches in America today have any approach of intentionality in reaching this group at key life points. But your church can be the exception.

From the Dechurched to the Unchurched

The book of Haggai, the only two-chapter book of the Bible, takes place in the years following the Babylonian exile of the Jews. When the Persians became the dominant power, they allowed the Jews to return to their homeland of Jerusalem. But the Jews found the city, the wall around the city, and the temple of God in ruins.

That remnant had a mandate from God to rebuild the temple. They were given all the resources they needed by the benevolent Persians. They began building the foundation of the house of God, but then their work came to a halt.

Haggai was God's prophetic spokesman. Through him the Jews heard from God for the first time since the exile. God's words through Haggai were indicting: "You expected much, but then it amounted to little. When you brought the harvest to your house, I ruined it. Why?" This is the declaration of the LORD of Hosts. "Because My house still lies in ruins, while each of you is busy with his own house" (Hag. 1:9).

God's people were commanded to build the temple. Instead, they chose to focus on their own comforts and desires. As a consequence God removed His blessings from the people.

We have been given the Great Commission to make disciples, to share the gospel, and to build God's house. But significant numbers of American churches and Christians are not being obedient. For many reasons we remain still and silent. And none of those reasons is acceptable to God.

The initial challenge of this research project was the dismal comments and statistics we recorded. Our churches are losing so many young adults that it could be disheartening. But the good news followed. We heard from young adults who returned to church after several years' absence. And we looked at churches that were effective in reaching, retaining, and reclaiming this group.

In the first part of this chapter, we shared about the young adults who had returned to church. For the remainder of the chapter, we will focus on those who have never or rarely been to church. We thus move from the dechurched to the unchurched.

Essential Churches That Reach the Unchurched

The young adult population not only is a significant number of dechurched America; they are also a large portion of unchurched America. When we began to examine essential churches, we found some fascinating similarities.

First, these churches had intentional efforts to retain those who were in the church. They tended to be better at assimilation and retention.

Second, the essential churches also directed their efforts at the reclamation of those who had dropped out of churches, not only their own churches but other churches as well. In other words, they directed much of their resources toward the dechurched.

Another similarity among the essential churches was their efforts to reach the lost and unchurched world, many of whom had never or rarely attended a church. In other words, the essential church was truly a multiplying church in a myriad of ways.

The unchurched can be found in all age groups, but the numbers increase with youth. Look at the percentage of four different generations who attend church each weekend:[3]

Who Attends Church in America Each Weekend?

Generation	Birth Years	Percentage Attending Church
Builders	Before 1946	51%
Boomers	1946 to 1964	41%
Busters	1965 to 1976	34%
Bridgers	1977 to 1994	29%

The growth of unchurched America is obvious. The younger the person, the greater is the likelihood that he or she will be unchurched. And the growing ranks of the unchurched are not due to problems related to certain geographical areas. For certain there are areas like Yolo County, California, in which only 28 percent of the residents are claimed by any church, probably because of the influence of alternative religions and the presence of the University of California, Davis. While we shake our heads knowingly that Yolo County is 72 percent unchurched, do we realize that rural areas like Menifee County, Kentucky (population 5,200), are 87 percent unchurched?[4]

Essential churches are multiplying churches. They seek to reach those who are not currently in church; and, often, they start new campuses and new churches. They are driven by a doctrine that compels them to reach those who do not know Christ.

Doctrine Really Matters . . . and Multiplies

In chapter 8 we looked at the issue of doctrine in the essential church. The process was called "deepen," and it referred to leading Christians to greater biblical depth and greater spiritual maturity. But in an ironic twist, our earlier research found that the *unchurched* were most attracted to churches that held a high view of Scripture and that taught matters of biblical depth.

We interviewed 353 formerly unchurched persons across America to hear what their perspectives of church were before they became Christians and before they became active in a church. Most of these formerly unchurched had been Christians for less than a year at the time of our interviews. And most of them had never been in a church prior to the year of the interview.

The surprise? Of these formerly unchurched, 91 percent told us that the doctrine of the church was important to them *before* they became Christians.[5] "Even before I became a Christian," Cheryl told us, "I was really interested in what churches believed. I had enough common sense to know they weren't all exactly alike. I wanted to find a church that could stick to its guns on its beliefs."

These formerly unchurched, however, weren't just interested in the facts of the doctrine; they were insistent that the churches should be uncompromising in their stand. These facts fly in the face of an increasingly pluralistic and theologically tolerant culture. It seems as if, when one takes the step from being firmly unchurched to at least becoming an inquirer, attitudes change. The seeker desires to discover truth and to see real conviction among Christians about the reality of God, Jesus, and the entire supernatural realm. Jorge spoke rather bluntly about the issue: "I visited a few churches before I became a Christian. Man, some of them made me want to vomit! They didn't show any more conviction about their beliefs than I did. And I was lost and going to hell!"

These formerly unchurched people were clear. They not only were interested in learning about doctrine; they were attracted to conservative, evangelical churches that were uncompromising in their beliefs.

Because nine out of ten formerly unchurched told us that doctrine was a major factor in their coming to church and, ultimately, becoming a Christian, we delved further into this issue. "Why," we asked, "is doctrine so important to you?" Their most frequent response was their desire to know absolutes in a culture that largely eschews absolutes.

Janet is a stay-at-home mom living in the Cincinnati area. She was raised in a home with no church background, and her parents are "friendly agnostics." Janet's parents never communicated any particular sense of truth to her. "I'm not sure on what authority they base their values."

Janet and Lyle married seven years ago, and they now have two sons. Janet expressed to Lyle her desire to find for their children some type of environment that had a clearly defined value system. Lyle had grown up attending a Southern Baptist church across the Ohio River in Kentucky. An affable fellow according to Janet, Lyle was glad to help her on this quest.

"I began my search for truth under the guise that my kids needed clear boundaries," Janet said. "But the search was really for me." Of course, neither Janet nor Lyle was a Christian at this point.

Janet described the frustration of her upbringing. "My parents didn't have a clue. The schools I attended, from kindergarten to college, seemed to have a disdain for absolutes. And all the friends I hung around were as clueless as I was. Here I was twenty-nine years old, and I felt like a kid lost in a big store."

Naturally religion and church were on Janet's mind as paths to pursue, but she really did not know where to turn. She was fortunate. The first church she and Lyle visited gave her the answers she had been seeking. "God was looking after me. I could have gone a thousand different directions, but I just remember seeing this church from the interstate and thinking that it looked nice," she reflected.

The church of choice was a warm, evangelical, nondenominational community church. Attendance was about six hundred, and the church put a lot of resources into its children's ministry. Both Matt and Brett, their sons, instantly connected with the church, and Janet knew she had found the perfect place right away.

"It was unbelievable. The church made clear their positions on doctrinal issues in their publications. Pastor Eric spoke clearly about the church's biblical position in his sermons. I had to decide that either all the people in the church were deluded or that I found the answers I was seeking. I chose the latter."

Janet and Lyle became followers of Christ a few weeks later. Doctrine had brought them to church, and it keeps them there today.

Thousands of conservative, evangelical churches believe the right doctrine with great conviction, but they are still losing young adults, and they are not reaching the unchurched world either.

While we found that right beliefs are critical in churches and Christians that multiply themselves, that alone is not sufficient. Right doctrine must be accompanied by right actions.

Don't Just Stand There; Do Something

If there is a single word that could best describe essential churches, it would be *intentional*. The churches and their leaders are intentional about having a church structure that aids the discipleship process rather than one that impedes it. They are intentional about moving Christians to a deeper walk with Christ with deeper teachings of the Bible. They believe the Bible without hesitation or reservation. And they are intentional about multiplying, reaching those who left the church and reaching those who are not Christians and who have never been in church.

When we are asked about the best method of outreach for a church, our typical response is, "Don't just stand there; do something." We are serious. Most of the churches in America do not reach the dechurched and the unchurched because they don't try. They just stand there.

These churches may have an occasional special event for the community. Or they may have a tired and dated outreach night where only a few people ever show up. But they are not consistent and persistent in reaching others. Note that we have not recommended any one method of outreach. In most churches anything would be better than the "nothing" that is taking place.

One of our evaluation instruments we use in our consultations is an "Unchurched-Reaching Readiness Inventory." We asked a number of churches to read the statements and to rate them on a scale of one to five, with the lowest score being "strongly disagree" and the highest score being "strongly agree." Below are some of the statements on the readiness inventory.

Our church has a strong desire to reach lost and unchurched people.

Many people in our church share their faith regularly.

Many people in our church develop relationships with unchurched people.

The people in our church are friendly to outsiders.

Our pastor has a passion to reach lost and unchurched people.

People in our church are unified; they do not tend to argue over minor issues.

An unchurched person would feel comfortable in our worship services.

Personal evangelism is a priority in our church.

We pray for lost and unchurched people by name.

An unchurched person would feel comfortable in a small group or Sunday school class in our church.

We have attempted many things to reach the unchurched.

We see many unchurched people reached for Christ in our church.

A significant portion of our church's growth comes from reaching the unchurched.

The total number of questions is fifty. By the time a member completes the inventory, he or she usually has a good idea how well the church will fare with the final results. Simply stated, most churches are not doing something; they are just standing there.

A Word about the Pastor and to the Pastor

We noted early in this book about the significant role of the pastor in essential churches. We shared our research about the dechurched and rechurched young adults, and how they look to "the main man" as an example and leader.

We are reluctant to speak more about the significant role the pastor plays in the church's becoming a multiplying church. So much responsibility has been placed on pastors that they often bear the brunt of too many criticisms for every little thing in the church. And frankly, some pastors withdraw toward inertia because they have been so abused, so criticized, and so nitpicked by people who call themselves Christians. They no longer feel that any effort is worth the pain.

One of us is a pastor (Sam), and other has been a pastor (Thom). We have both dealt with some not-so-well-intentioned dragons in the church. Sometimes it is easier to do nothing than to do something and be verbally crucified.

Nevertheless, pastors must lead their churches to multiply, to reach others—especially this young adult group that is leaving at an alarming rate. These leaders must not quit the fight. Too much is at stake. Eternity is in the balance. Yes, too much pressure is placed on pastors. Certainly unreasonable expectations abound. But this battle is a part of a larger war. It is indeed spiritual warfare.

Pastors, be people of prayer. Seek God's face. Strive to reach and keep people, especially this young adult group that we are losing. Lead your church to something so great that it will be a certain failure unless God is in it. Dream the big dream. Dream God's dream for your church.

When Young Adults Get on Board . . .

We remind you of the major reason young adults drop out of the church: they do not see church as essential to their lives. They left because they simply wanted a break from church (27 percent). They left when they moved to college and didn't think finding a new church was worth the effort (25 percent). They let work responsibilities come before church (23 percent). They left because they moved too far away from church but did not bother to find a closer church (22 percent). And they left because they were just too busy (22 percent).

You get the picture. They just did not consider church essential to their lives.

Sometimes the solution is to find ways to do more for these young adults. "If we can just offer them things that make them happy," we reason, "they won't leave the church." But the reality is that most young adults don't just want more done for *them*. They want to do more for *others*. And nowhere is this more apparent than those times a young adult gets involved in reaching out to others. The young adult becomes part of the multiplying church.

"Our church took a real chance," Dawn shared with us. Dawn is a member of a church in Michigan with three hundred average attendance. "The local hospice organization asked our ministry staff to assist them with some hospice visits. The staff helped, but they saw the need to expand the ministry to others in the church. The student pastor suggested something really radical for most churches. He said we should get the high school students involved in the ministry." Dawn was one of those students.

"We had a core high school group of about twenty-five," Dawn continued. "When the student pastor made the proposal, the first question someone asked was, 'What is hospice?' Then he told us that it was ministry and practical help for terminally ill people. You could have heard a pin drop."

The students heard a presentation by a hospice leader, and twelve of the students volunteered to be trained. Then it came time for their first visits.

"I was scared to death," Dawn confessed. "Even though I was with a hospice professional who promised to do all the talking, I was still scared. Our first visit was to a thirty-eight-year-old woman in the latter stages of cancer. I'm not even sure what type of cancer it was. The point was that she was dying, and I had never been around someone dying before. It broke my heart to see her eight- and ten-year-old daughters. But I fell in love with those girls after several weeks."

Dawn would make several visits to several terminal patients. Though she never felt fully comfortable, she did adjust. "I did some things for some of those women (all of my visits were to females) that I never dreamed I would do for anyone. Then Marcy died."

Marcy was the young mother whom Dawn first visited. Dawn was tearful, but she continued. "I told Marcy about Jesus before she died, and she accepted Jesus. The family asked me to speak at her funeral. It just blew me away. I told how she had accepted Jesus and how happy I was that she was in heaven. And get this: I was sixteen years old at the time!"

Why did we repeat Dawn's story? We wanted to provide a living illustration of a young person who never dropped out of church. Today, at age twenty-three, Dawn is still active and growing spiritually in her church. And she credits her involvement and ministry to hospice patients as the key to moving toward a greater commitment for Christ and, thus, for the church.

The young people in our churches are not content to be on the sidelines. They desire to be involved in ministries that reach out to the community and the world. They want to be in churches that will take faith risks and get them involved in real life-changing ministries. They are not loyal to the institution for the sake of the institution, but they are loyal to institutions that are making a difference and institutions where they can make a difference.

Nearly two-thirds (65 percent) of young adults who did *not* drop out of church between the ages of eighteen and twenty-two viewed church as a vital part of their relationship with God. "That's what I learned in the hospice ministry," Dawn affirmed. "I can't be the Christian I need to be apart from the church. I discovered how the body of Christ is supposed to work. That's probably why I am still in church today."

Another four out of ten (42 percent) young adults stayed with the church because they were committed to the purpose and the work of the church. "I believe in what my church does," Dawn said, "because I have been on the front lines of ministry. There is no better way to believe in a cause than to be involved in it."

Essential Churches: Looking Outward

Essential churches are multiplying churches because they constantly seek to look and reach beyond themselves. They thus multiply with the presence of new Christians and with the return of the dechurched. Many are multiplying churches because they start new churches, new campuses, and new ministries. That outward focus attracts and retains young adults. They want to be a part of something that is making a difference.

Simplify. Deepen. Expect. Multiply.

We have shared with you a plethora of statistics and data. We have looked at the plight of the exodus of young adults from our churches. And we have shared four major facets of those essential churches that reach, reclaim, and retain young adults.

Simplify. Deepen. Expect. Multiply.

That sounds basic enough, but what does it really look like? What are some practical things an essential church would do today?

We're glad you asked. We will respond in the next chapter.

Building an Essential Church: A Case Study

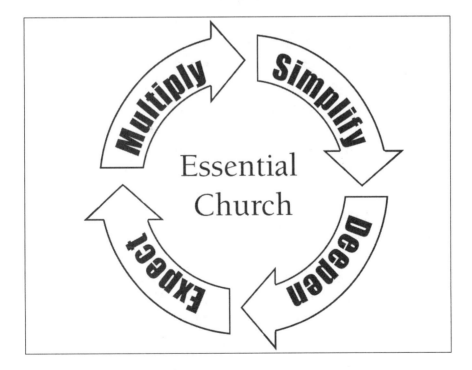

When it is all said and done, when the research is complete and the book is written, we inevitably hear the question: How does this apply to my church? It is a good question. It is the right question. Leaders are wise in realizing that, while the Word of God is unchanging, contextual issues make every church unique. That is why we eschew the cookie-cutter approach to church health.

Such an approach has two faulty assumptions. First, it can be man-centered instead of God-centered. The danger in books, conferences, and other instructional tools is that the focus can easily shift from a dependence on God to a dependence on the methodology. We all know numerous examples where the latest thing in church growth and church health became the hot fad that many church leaders attempted to emulate.

A second fallacious assumption to the cookie-cutter approach is that all churches are alike, or at least they are similar. Such an assumption ignores the uniqueness of every congregation and the uniqueness of the community in which the church is located.

We receive hundreds, if not thousands, of requests to give examples of how an approach might work in a church so we do just that in this chapter. We do so with caution and reservations. If our case study becomes *the* way many churches become essential churches, then we have failed. We did not present this plethora of information on church dropouts and these overarching themes to suggest that there is a single way to become an essential church. So we offer you one possible example.

We believe that our major themes are well supported. Many churches have become busy with activities, with seemingly no God-given strategic reasons to explain why they do what they do. Thus we encourage churches to *simplify*.

We also have a wealth of data to demonstrate the growing biblical ignorance among Christians in America. And we think we have made a good case to demonstrate that such illiteracy has been a major contributor to the high dropout rates of eighteen- to twenty-two-year-olds. Thus we encourage churches to *deepen*.

The importance of church is diminishing among Christians in our nation. Almost any aggregate statistics on the church will support that reality. Churches across America have dumbed down what it means to be a part of a local congregation. Thus we encourage churches to *expect* more of their members.

With present trends continuing, the American church will die. The process of dying may be slow and agonizing, but churches are still dying. Conversions are down precipitously. The number of new churches started is having trouble keeping up with the number of churches that are dying. And we still have a huge need for churches to be more missional in their neighborhoods and in distant lands. Thus we encourage churches to *multiply*.

We offer the following fictitious case study, trusting that you will understand our heart's desire not to present a cookie-cutter approach. And though the church and its context are fictitious, we can point to many similar churches in many similar contexts that look and act a lot like Clear Springs Community Church. Maybe you will see some of your church in the story as well.

Clear Springs Community Church

Clear Springs Community Church began in 1962 as Clear Springs Baptist Mission, a new church start of First Baptist. The church became autonomous in 1965, and the name changed to Clear Springs Baptist Church. In 1999 Clear Springs dropped its denominational name and has been in ministry under its present name since then.

The church has experienced some growth, but most of it is in spurts. It grew to 110 in worship attendance from 1962 to 1965 but grew little for the next decade. From 1976 to 1983, under the leadership of a new pastor, the church doubled in size and acquired new property and added significantly to the church facilities. The average attendance of 220 to 250 stabilized from 1983 to 1994. During that period Clear Springs had three pastors and several contentious moments among church members. The primary argument was over relocation, as several leaders tried to get the church to relocate from its present five-acre site. All attempts to relocate failed.

In 1995 the church had an unexpected blessing when someone joined the congregation who owned seven acres adjacent to the church. Before the year was over, he had donated the entire property valued at $1.4 million. The church now had twelve acres, a new pastor, and a new attitude. For the next ten years the church experienced steady but not spectacular growth. Average attendance was 275. The current pastor came to the church in 2004, and the attendance still ranges between 260 and 290.

The church is located in a Midwestern town with a population of twenty-eight thousand. The demographics are largely middle-class Anglos although the Hispanic population now accounts for 10 percent of the total and is the only growing demographic group.

Clear Springs Community Church has actually received 570 new members over the past ten years although the average attendance grew by only fifty during that same time period. Stated simply, the back door is wide open. The largest exodus, like many churches, is with the young adults ages eighteen to twenty-two.

The church has good facilities and ample land for future growth. It is not experiencing significant financial problems although the congregation did lower its mission support from 10 percent of budget to 8 percent of budget. The church has three full-time ministers: a senior pastor, a worship pastor, and a student pastor. They also have two half-time ministers: one serving as education minister and one serving as preschool and children's minister.

The pastor is frustrated. Even though the community is not experiencing significant growth, two-thirds of the population is unchurched. A new Hispanic service has helped, but the potential is still unmet. Pastor Glenn wonders if he made a mistake by moving his family here. More than the lack of numerical growth, however, he is almost despondent at what he perceives to be a lack of spiritual growth among the members. He knows that many members go out the back door due to spiritual immaturity. And Clear Springs Community Church has done little to help them grow spiritually.

In an extended prayer time one morning, Pastor Glenn asked God to help him lead the church to be the kind of church that pleases God. He did not ask for specific items, just to be a God-pleasing church. Though he heard no audible voice and though he did not know what would take place next, he left his prayer time with a greater confidence that his work at Clear Springs is not yet done.

Over the next two years, the church experienced a slow but significant transformation. Attendance is growing slowly, but the back door is closing more each month. Many leaders in the church note with joy the spiritual growth that is taking place among many members. Indeed the church seems to be finding a new purpose and, consequently, has a new attitude.

The story of Clear Springs Community Church does not receive much recognition beyond the community. It is not a fast-growing church, and its average attendance of 320 certainly does not make it one of the larger churches in the nation.

But the leaders of the church know that something has taken place. They know that it is not the same church it was two years ago. And though they realize that the church has a long way to go, they look with excitement at the path they are following.

What happened at Clear Springs Community Church? The church has become more essential to the lives of its members. As a consequence the members are growing spiritually, and more people outside of the church are being reached. Let's unpack the transformation of the past two years. The following developments did not necessarily take place sequentially, but the leaders can point to four major steps: simplify, deepen, expect, and multiply.

The Simplification of Clear Springs Community Church

Like many, perhaps most, churches in America, Clear Springs was a busy church with a lot of activities and a lot of meetings. Pastor Glenn and the ministry staff formed a strategic vision task force and began addressing the issue.

The purpose statement. "OK," Pastor Glenn said in an early meeting of the task force, "what would we like to see happen to a member of our church? When someone joins our church, for example, what do we tell them they should expect?"

The lively discussion lasted two hours, and more discussions took place over the next several weeks. The group finally arrived at a consensus. They wanted members to worship God corporately. They wanted them to grow spiritually. They desired to see that members connect with other members. And they wanted them to be involved in some type of ministry reaching out to others.

They decided that they would capture the thoughts in four simple words: *worship, deepen, connect,* and *reach.* They were amazed. Instead of trying to develop a purpose or mission statement and then letting the slogan die on a wall or a banner, they decided to let the development of disciples drive the purpose statement.

The purpose statement becomes the discipleship process. Before they took the concept to the entire church, the leadership team began to think how this purpose statement would actually flesh out. They worked again for many hours and concluded with this concept:

1. *Worship*—Members should be in the worship service each week.
2. *Deepen*—Through the sermons, weekly attendance at a Sunday morning Bible study, and attending at least one

six-week discipleship class each week, members would grow in their faith.

3. *Connect*—Members would best connect with other members in the Sunday morning Bible study since it is an open, ongoing group.
4. *Reach*—Members would become involved in at least one outreach ministry or mission trip each year.

When the purpose statement and the discipleship process were shared with the entire congregation over several weeks, the enthusiasm began to grow. Joe Barber, a charter member of the church, stated it well: "I love this purpose statement because it not only says who we are but also what we do. I can tell anyone that what we do at Clear Springs is worship, deepen, connect, and reach."

The church aligned its ministries with the purpose statement. The next step involved looking at all of the busyness of the church. Some of the ministries were obvious fits. The Sunday morning Bible study was part of the "deepen and connect" in the discipleship process. And their experience with the Christmas Eve service was supported by research that said it was the number one event that the unchurched attend. So they kept that big event as part of the "reach" component. Instead of random mission trips, they started working with their Hispanic members to take mission trips to their homelands. Of course, that strategic move was part of the "reach" component as well.

The church eliminated some ministries that they could not align. When the church began to assess all of its activities honestly, the members saw that many of their activities did not really contribute to the purpose and the discipleship process. Five committees had not met in three years so that decision of elimination was easy. But it got tough after that.

The leaders discovered several "sacred cows" that were difficult to eliminate. With two of them, the leaders were able to redirect some people to other areas so the conflict was minimal. With several, however, the elimination would have brought severe conflict to the church.

Doris Caylor, a five-year member and a leader on the vision team, made a proposal to the leadership group. "Folks, let's don't put our church through more conflict. Let these members continue to have their ministries that don't align with other discipleship processes. I think they will likely die a natural death."

Her words proved prophetic. Within two years all but three of the "sacred cows" were gone.

The Deepening of Clear Springs Community Church

Pastor Glenn knew that the spiritual growth of the members of Clear Springs began with his example. He gathered a group of trusted friends in the church and shared with them his thoughts.

The pastor gave greater attention to his sermons. "Guys," Pastor Glenn began, "if we are really expecting spiritual growth from our members when they come to the worship services, I have to do a better job preaching. I'll be honest with you. I'm not spending nearly enough time in sermon preparation. I've gotten so busy doing other church stuff that I'm neglecting one of the most important things I do."

The friends appreciated the pastor's candor. They started making suggestions on how he could better spend his ministry days, and they offered to protect him when the inevitable criticisms came when he did not make an appearance at every expected event.

Pastor Glenn did not easily make the transition. His pastor heart wanted to be with the members every time they asked for him. And the occasional criticism for not being at an event stung him. The pastor saw his progress as "three steps forward and two steps backward," but he slowly began increasing his time in God's Word and sermon preparation.

The church developed open Bible study groups. The vision team was particularly excited about the role of open Bible study groups. "Open" refers to the type of small group. It means that the group is ongoing with no planned closing. A person can join the group at any point; thus this form of small group has real outreach potential since a member can invite someone to join them on any given week.

Open groups also help members to connect with each other in Christian fellowship as some people will stay in the same group for months or even years.

The church also made the decision to study Bible books. They decided on a curriculum series called Explore the Bible, which went through the entire Bible in seven-year cycles, alternating each three months between Old Testament books and New Testament books. Pastor Glenn got so excited about the study that he decided to do most of his preaching on the same texts used in Explore the Bible.

The church used closed groups for further discipleship study. A closed group has an established length of existence at the beginning. Clear Springs Community Church decided to ask all of their small-group leaders, other than the open-group leaders, to limit the duration of the group to six one-week sessions.

Because members were only expected to be in one or two of these six-week groups a year, many could be offered without pressuring people to attend all of them. Some of them would take place at the church; others would continue in homes; and still others could be in restaurants, Starbucks, and other neutral sites.

Already the members were talking about the wide variety of small groups and the way the groups would help them grow as Christians. "I have several Muslim coworkers," Susie Franklin said. "I plan to get in the first group that has an overview of Islam.

There is then another group later in the year that will give highlights on the Koran."

"I can't wait to get into one of the Christian doctrine groups," Elmer Jansen commented. "I want to learn more about the doctrine of the Trinity."

Greater sermon preparation time for the pastor. Open groups. Closed groups. The momentum was growing.

The church began to encourage more personal Bible study. The leaders of the church determined that the church would "deepen" if members were taught well during the sermons, if they were in small-group Bible studies, and if they studied the Bible alone and personally. In order to encourage the latter, the church made available on its Web site daily Bible readings that matched what would be taught in the open Bible study the following Sunday morning. Thus the members were studying the same passages personally, in groups, and, most of the time, hearing sermons preached on those same texts.

Raising the Expectations at Clear Springs Community Church

The leaders of the church realized, early in the transformation plans, that change would not take place overnight. The church, throughout its history, had been a low-expectation church. Membership was no more than adding a name to a roll.

But they didn't want to make the same mistakes other churches had made. They spoke with several leaders of other churches who had gone to an extreme to develop a high-expectation church. Membership had become a cumbersome and discouraging process. And what began as high expectations evolved into legalism.

Clear Springs Community Church strove for balance. After two years the leadership felt positive about the direction the church was headed.

The church established a four-hour membership class. The leaders knew that new members should come through a membership class. That is the entry level where expectations are shared and where information about the church is provided. A membership class was absolutely necessary.

They learned lessons from other churches that had gone overboard with membership classes. Some lasted for weeks. Others had multiple courses and a plethora of inventories and surveys to take.

Clear Springs knew that much of what takes place in membership classes in some churches today really belongs in a discipleship class. The membership class is an introduction, not indoctrination. The church thus decided to make the class four hours, all in one setting, offered at different times throughout the year.

The church used the membership class to establish expectations at the onset of membership. The leaders of Clear Springs realized that expectations must be established early. More than one-half of the two hours of the membership class was devoted to establishing those expectations through the purpose statement: Worship, Deepen, Connect, Reach.

New members often laughed that they heard the purpose statement a hundred times in four hours, but they left understanding the statement. They left understanding the process of discipleship, and they left understanding what was expected of them.

The church used video testimonies to encourage expectations. At least once a month during Sunday morning worship service, the congregation would hear from a member who was sold out on the purpose statement and whose own life was being transformed by his or her growth as a disciple of Christ. These testimonies encourage others to stay faithful to the mission of the church.

The pastor intentionally used the sermons to encourage expectations. On several occasions in the course of a year, the pastor would relate the biblical text of his sermon to the purpose statement of the church. On other occasions he would use a story about a church member, with permission, that spoke of life change in his or her discipleship growth. The sermons became powerful reminders to the congregation about the purpose and the mission of the church.

The Multiplication of Clear Springs Community Church

Pastor Glenn believes that Clear Springs has a long way to go in this facet of becoming an essential church. He looks at the facts—no more than twenty-five conversions each of the past two years—and he knows that much more should and can be done. But the Great Commission atmosphere is changing for the better at the church, and he is hopeful that better days are on the way.

The church is encouraging members to invite others, especially to the open Bible study groups. This approach is low-key, but it does seem to be having a positive impact. The number of guests to the worship services is increasing, but so is the number of guests in the open groups. And the leadership of the church has noticed that guests in the open groups are more likely to become a part of the congregation. Of course, they knew that would be the case since the guests are immediately connecting with members in the open groups.

The church leaders are well aware of the power of simply inviting people, especially if the church member actually brings someone to church. And not only is the church attracting the unchurched through the power of the invitation, but some dechurched members are returning as well. This response corresponds with the research that showed one-half of the dechurched who returned to church did so as the result of encouragement from family or friends.

The pastor is setting the example in personal evangelism. One of the highest correlated factors in evangelistic churches is the commitment of the pastor to do personal evangelism. Pastor Glenn knows that this research applies to him and Clear Springs. He holds himself accountable to two men each week for his own personal evangelistic activity.

Many of the members are noticing. And some of those members are beginning to follow the lead of their pastor.

The church is involved in strategic mission trips led by their Hispanic members into countries where they lived. It seemed to be common sense once they made the decision. Right in their midst were people who could lead mission trips into areas they knew best. After all, most of them lived in these countries just a few years ago. The Hispanics in the congregation also know where the greatest needs are. Resources of people, time, and money are now used for most efficient stewardship.

The church is participating in church-planting efforts. One of those efforts takes place on the international mission trips. The other is a partnership with two other churches to start a church just twenty miles away in the same county.

The Essential Church

Pastor Glenn now has an excitement about Clear Springs Community Church. He no longer wonders if he made a mistake by coming to the church. Most of his days are filled with excitement and anticipation. One of the greatest joys he expressed was the dramatic reduction in the dropout rate among the eighteen- to twenty-two-year-old young adults in the church.

Sure he still has some tough days. Ministry always has its struggles. And he still has his critics. For some reason some people would rather be a part of a dying church than to make the necessary changes to be an essential church.

Can your church become just like Clear Springs Community Church? Absolutely not! No two churches are alike, and no two communities are alike. But your church can move toward becoming a congregation that is vital to the members. Your church can be moved to simplify, deepen, expect, and multiply. And your church can see more people reached with the gospel of Christ.

We truly believe that it is possible to reduce the outflow of young adults from our churches. Two-thirds of the people in this age group are leaving our churches. But the good news is that most of them would like to find a church that is healthy, a church that wants more than business as usual.

They are looking for churches where they can make a difference. They are looking for churches that are making a difference.

They are looking for essential churches.

May God make it so in your church.

About the Authors

Thom S. Rainer is the president and CEO of LifeWay Christian Resources, one of the largest Christian resource companies in the world. He has consulted with more than five hundred churches, served as a pastor in four churches and interim pastor in seven churches, and spoken in hundreds of venues around the world. His publications include nineteen books and hundreds of articles. He and his wife, Nellie Jo, live in Nashville. They have three grown sons: Sam, Art, and Jess.

Sam S. Rainer III serves the church as a senior pastor. He is a frequent speaker on church health issues. He also serves as the president and CEO of Rainer Research. He has extensive experience in church and denominational research and is the author of numerous articles on the church as well as the coauthor of this book. Sam also has worked in a consulting role for Fortune 1000 companies. In addition, he writes a regular column for *Outreach* magazine, and his blog is found at http://churchforward.outreachmagazine.com. For consulting and/or research, contact him at www.RainerResearch.com. Sam is married to Erin.

Notes

Introducing the Essential Church

1. "A Resurgence Not Yet Realized," Thom Rainer; derived from LifeWay ACP data.

2. See www.cia.gov/library/publications/the-world-factbook/fields/2122. html.

3. Original research by Rainer Research, May 2007, "R.E.A.Ch. Buildings."

4. C. H. Spurgeon, *The Soul Winner: How to Lead Sinners to the Saviour* (Grand Rapids, MI: Wm. B. Eerdmans Publishing Co., 1963), 17.

5. See www.online.wsj.com/article/SB118434936941966055. html?mod=googlenews_wsj.

6. See www.census.gov.

7. Rebecca Barnes and Lindy Lowry, "The American Church in Crisis," *Outreach*, May/June 2006.

8 Ibid.

9. LifeWay Research survey, part 1 original research, "How Many Leave Church between Ages 18-22 and Why?"

10. See www.sbclife.com/Articles/2004/02/SLA4.asp.

11. See www.census.gov/Press-Release/www/releases/archives/ population/010048.html.

My Faith Is Not My Parents' Faith

1. LifeWay Research survey, part 1 original research, "How Many Leave Church between Ages 18–22 and Why?"

2. Ibid.

3. LifeWay Research survey, part 3 original research, "Faces of Young Adults ages 18–22: The Effect of Church Dropouts."

4. See www.usatoday.com/news/religion/2007–12–17-student-spirituality_N. htm.

5. Ibid.

6. See hosted.ap.org/dynamic/stories/Y/YOUTH_POLL_SPIRITUALITY?SIT E=RIPAW&SECTION=HOME&TEMPLATE=DEFAULT.

7. See www.lifeway.com/lwc/article_main_page/0%2C1703%2CA%25253D16 5950%252526M%25253D200906%2C00.html.

8. LifeWay Research survey, part 3 original research, "Faces of Young Adults Ages 18–22: The Effect of Church Dropouts."

9. LifeWay Research survey, part 2 original research, "Teen Influences on Church Dropouts."

10. See www.lifeway.com/lwc/article_main_page/0%2C1703%2CA%25253D1 65950%252526M%25253D200906%2C00.html.

11. See www.hosted.ap.org/dynamic/stories/Y/YOUTH_POLL_SPIRITUALI TY?SITE=RIPAW&SECTION=HOME&TEMPLATE=DEFAULT.

Looking for a Different Kind of Community

1. See users1.wsj.com/lmda/do/checkLogin?mg=wsj-users1&url=http%3A%2F%2Fonline.wsj.com%2Farticle%2FSB11607053909929151 4.html.

2. See en.wikipedia.org/wiki/Community.

3. LifeWay Research survey, part 3 original research, "Faces of Young Adults Ages 18–22: The Effect of Church Dropouts."

4. See www.antiochsheffield.org/CHFBC_ppt.ppt. Autumn Davis' story used with her permission.

5. See www.namb.net/site/apps/nl/content2.asp?c=9qKILUOzEpH&b=16485 83&ct=3257571.

6. Rainer Group original contracted research. "R.E.A.Ch." Buildings 2007.

7. Charles MacKay, *Extraordinary Popular Delusions and the Madness of Crowds* (reprint, New York: Barnes and Noble Books, 1993), 89.

8. See en.wikipedia.org/wiki/Third_place.

9. Rainer Research original contracted research. "R.E.A.Ch." Buildings 2007 and Rainer Group original contracted research "F.I.R.St" 2005.

10. Ibid.

11. LifeWay Research survey, part 1 original research, "How Many Leave Church between Ages 18–22 and Why?"

12. Ibid.

13. Ibid.

That's Life! It Changes

1. See www.bls.gov/tus/charts/home.htm.

2. See www.engadget.com/2007/01/23/shocker-americans-spend-more-time-with-pc-than-spouse/.

3. See usgovinfo.about.com/od/censusandstatistics/a/commutetimes.htm.

4. LifeWay Research survey, part 3 original research, "Faces of Young Adults Ages 18–22: The Effect of Church Dropouts."

5. See www.factfinder.census.gov/servlet/STTable?_bm=y&-geo_id=01000US
&-qr_name=ACS_2006_EST_G00_S0101&-ds_name=ACS_2006_EST_G00_.

6. Ibid.

7. Chuck Lawless, *Membership Matters* (Grand Rapids, MI: Zondervan, 2005), 48.

8. LifeWay Research survey, part 2 original research, "Teen Influences on Church Dropouts."

9. Ibid.

10. Ibid.

11. See www.christianpost.com/article/20070614/27982_College_
Not_%27Public_Enemy%27_for_Religiosity%2C_Study_Shows.htm.

12. Ibid.

A New Spin on Hypocrisy

1. LifeWay Research survey, part 2 original research, "Teen Influences on Church Dropouts."

2. Ibid.

3. Ibid.

4. Ibid.

5. Ibid.

6. David Kinnaman, *unChristian* (Grand Rapids, MI: Baker Books, 2007), 53.

7. Ibid, 48.

8. LifeWay Research survey, part 3 original research, "Faces of Young Adults Ages 18–22: The Effect of Church Dropouts."

9. Ibid.

All Eyes on the Main Man

1. LifeWay Research survey, part 1 original research, "How Many Leave Church between Ages 18–22 and Why?"

2. See en.wikipedia.org/wiki/Willard_Vandiver.

3. LifeWay Research survey, part 2 original research, "Teen Influences on Church Dropouts."

4. See www.cnn.com/2004/SHOWBIZ/TV/04/12/roulette.win.

5. LifeWay Research survey, part 2 original research, "Teen Influences on Church Dropouts."

6. Donald A. McGavran, *Understanding Church Growth* (Grand Rapids, MI: Eerdmans, 1980), 225.

7. LifeWay Research survey, part 2 original research, "Teen Influences on Church Dropouts."

8. LifeWay Research survey, part 3 original research, "Faces of Young Adults Ages 18–22: The Effect of Church Dropouts."

9. LifeWay Research survey, part 1 original research, "How Many Leave Church between Ages 18–22 and Why?"

10. Ibid.

11. LifeWay Research survey, part 3 original research, "Faces of Young Adults Ages 18–22: The Effect of Church Dropouts."

The Essential Church and the Back Door

1.LifeWay Research survey, part 1 original research, "How Many Leave Church between Ages 18–22 and Why?"

2. See the following books by Thom S. Rainer: *Simple Church* (coauthored with Eric Geiger) (Nashville: B&H Publishing, 2006); *The Unchurched Next Door* (Grand Rapids: Zondervan, 2003); *Surprising Insights from the Unchurched* (Grand Rapids: Zondervan, 2001); *High Expectations* (Nashville: B&H Publishing, 1997); *Effective Evangelistic Churches* (Nashville: B&H Publishing, 1996).

3. Thom S. Rainer, *High Expectations* (Nashville: B&H Publishing, 1997).

Simplify: Getting the Structure Right

1. Thom S. Rainer and Eric Geiger, *Simple Church* (Nashville: B&H Publishing, 2006).

2. Alan Deutschman, "Change or Die," *Fast Company* 94 (May 2005), 54–62.

3. Tom Peters, *The Circle of Innovation* (New York: Random House, 1997), 37.

Deepen: Getting the Content Right

1. "A Resurgence Not Yet Realized," Thom Rainer, derived from LifeWay Annual Church Profile data.

Expect: Getting the Attitude Right

1. Thom S. Rainer, *High Expectations* (Nashville: Broadman & Holman, 1999).

2. Ibid., 141.

3. Thom S. Rainer and Eric Geiger, *Simple Church* (Nashville: B&H Publishing Group, 2006).

4. Rainer, *High Expectations*, 29–47.

5. Ibid., 44–45.

6. Ibid., 110.

Multiply: Getting the Action Right

1. Thom S. Rainer, *The Unchurched Next Door* (Grand Rapids, MI: Zondervan, 2003), 79.

2. Ibid., 267.

3. Thom S. Rainer, *Surprising Insights from the Unchurched* (Grand Rapids, MI: Zondervan, 2001), 34.

4. Ibid.

5. Ibid., 126.

essential church retreat
with LifeWay President Thom S. Rainer and Pastor Sam S. Rainer III

why do many people drop out of churches today?

Because, simply put, church is not an essential part of their lives.

That was the main finding of Thom Rainer and his son, Sam, as they talked to church dropouts to find out why they left and why some came back. They also looked at the churches that brought them back and those that had high retention rates. Four common disciplines emerged that these "essential" churches practice—simplify, deepen, expect, and multiply.

These are covered in the Rainer's new book *Essential Church*. But now, you can hear firsthand from the authors at the premier Essential Church Retreat.

Through four individual sessions, the Rainers will discuss the four critical actions of an essential church. Breakouts will follow after each session, so you can take that knowledge and brainstorm new ideas with like-minded peers who are facing similar challenges to yours. You'll also get time to meet with your own staff to develop new objectives for implementing the principles and strategies of *Essential Church* in your church.

LifeWay Ridgecrest Conference Center
February 26–28, 2009 – $299*

To find out more, visit www.lifeway.com/essentialchurch. Space is limited, so register your church staff soon. E-mail ridgecrest@lifeway.com or call 1.800.588.7222.

www.lifeway.com/essentialchurch

LifeWay | Leadership

* Early registration price per person: includes meals, lodging, and conference fees and materials. Registration cost after February 19 is $359.